The Sav... ...
New Netherlands

The Savior of New Netherlands

a poetry cycle in six chapters

Mac Oliver

LEAKY BOOT PRESS

The Savior of New Netherlands: a poetry cycle in six chapters
by Mac Oliver

Acknowledgments

Thanks to flashpointmag.com
and Grant, Maeve, Olivia, Seamus & Liam

First published in 2019 by
Leaky Boot Press
http://www.leakyboot.com

ISBN: 978-1-909849-68-6

For Peter Cooley & Paolo Valesio
Poets

The stone from which he rises up—and—ho,
The step to the bleaker depths of his descents...
　　　—Wallace Stevens, *The Rock*

Who reads me, when I am ashes,
Is my nephew in wishes
—Henry Adams, preface to *Mont-Saint-Michel & Chartres*

Fit & noble island fray, this story
Hears its audience in you

Contents

Chapter 3

We Stood Together

Chapter 4

Amid the Excavations

Chapter One

ADVENT

December 2005, Lower Manhattan

No Choice But to Negotiate

As one astray amid woods petrified,
A figure recognizable, who by
A twist returned to log the straits through which
There was no choice but to negotiate
His way, to tell what beckoned him get lost
At last & quit his silent questioning,
To speak aloud in lines of poetry,
For all the numbers bound to back away,
Remain beneath the tyranny of prose.

Lower Manhattan's a theatre wherein
You've seen the folly & the fraud play out,
As episodes a syndicate repeats.
I have pronounced, coerced, the shibboleths
With heavy tongue (a ruminant's),
Reviewed the tags affixed mistakenly.
You've seen (how could you not have seen) the waste
Exceed the ancient dynasties & cried
Along with others under burdens customs
Order you to bear, weighed in again,
A soul deprived of sun by edifices
In between its warmth & you at work,
Still held in high regard, despite how low
You've sunk, for productivity. But now,
Fed up with sloganeering, platitudes
The despots use to hide, misallocating
Through their final acts, I've found the nerve
To share unnerving news, & will in verse,
Should you come too, convey
The revolution of a consciousness

Beneath the shades of mammoth offices,
Recount how I, Ham Underhill, a temp,
Underemployed, a squatter, pockets all
But emptied, uninsurable, my clock
Just punched, was stopped mid-step, a rude
Awakening for this somnambulist
Who winds up automated by the day,
A kind of winter's nap, a daytime sleep
Just deep enough to see you miss
Foreshadowing of news to come,
As when attention spans divide for lack
Of focus, miss what's really happening.

A Strike

The gist is this: my tried routine was thwarted
When I found the flight of stairs
Descending to the *Uptown Local* blocked—
Police Line, Do Not Cross. It was a strike,
The city's transit union threatening
To shut the shopping season down, to use
Their leverage, & then went through with it,
Their picket lines to interrupt the cheer,
A high stakes tactic, surely, not to be
Ignored. That day I overheard a few
Executives refer to blackmail,
Their bonuses say seven times, or even
Seventy times seven times the best
Of transit salaries. I listen as
One mocks all strikes as mere ingratitude,
Just greed. I might have said that's spoken like
A real manager, well-paid. I ceased
To listen, each with beams in both his eyes,
To get another raise the goal with which
They are entirely preoccupied.
I'd say in retrospect, you take a side,
Whoever wins this round, who benefits
The most, but one who's honest must concede,
It's not a living to be envied, underground.

Both Await

"It's adventitious," was my second thought,
This transit strike, forced pivoting.
Now here's your chance to lose the hurried press
Of hustlers brawling, bustling from Wall,
An interruption much appreciated,
Like a gift as rare as myrrh, to find
You may advance by dawdling, unwind.
That night would be the longest of the year
Save one, the following. A hard dull cold
Came on but I decided not to troop
Towards home, or linger for a ride
Requiring so steep a fare as taxis
Charge, my money put aside for pit stops,
Wells to be determined on the way.
The wind went through my threadbare hand-me-downs,
Too thin for wind-chill such as this, their wool
Worn out, inadequate to cut the sheer
Exposure from the east, which triggers gusts
Accelerating up the narrow streets
Downtown, as if the banks were turbines,
Harnessing each one into a howl,
As if through all this strife an owl screeched
Its phrase to haunt an outcast settler,
Alone, ignorable, the elements
His match. Meanwhile, imagine hosts of dives
Behind whose heavy wooden doors you'd hear
The history revised, how they would quench
Deep thirst for warmth & light, where benches drenched
In both await, the bars one only notes on foot.

Somewhere Unheralded

Glazed eyes must squint away these gusts, as one
Grows icicles for eyelashes, like tinsel
On an ornamented spruce. You would
Have seen & heard me shivering at first,
Fists clenched, before I laughed it off & scoffed
At cowardice or lack of will I'd felt
On prior nights less cold than this instead
Of braving it & getting lost; instead
Of seeking out the seediest of spots
Because they're there, what reason else, & for
They're welcoming & cast an inner glow
Into the glut of outer dark; instead
Of generating heat within myself:
Defeated nights, locked in, long nights closed off
Spent muttering of permanent retreats,
Unbearably restricted, paralyzed.

This night I would resist, make liberty
My principle. I'd proudly lollygag,
Persist in getting lost, if possible,
Ignore the clock, nowhere to go, let thoughts
Of speed dissolve, forget the fidgeting
Of traders, edgy, frantic, finished off
For good. I'd make this leg on foot, despite
The distances involved, without the least
Regret I'd have to walk, console myself
It might have been a choice before, but I
Was always drifting off by now from all
The office shuffling, the tunneled heat.
So though I couldn't choose but walk—the strike

Deciding for me—pace, direction, those
Remained my choice, by indirection on
The way, with generally northward drift.
I had a hunch somewhere unheralded
Awaited me, some hidden nick beneath
A chimney made of brick, hospitable
Amid this chiseled schist, this mica schist
And gneiss I've missed when forced to rush the gate,
Through stop & go by sortilege of lights
That switched from green to red from street to street,
No time to pause for an extended look,
As when a restless passenger, no book
To open for escape, beneath the ground,
Pressed close to others, strap to steady me,
I met no other's pair of eyes, but rather
Studied all the pairs of leather shoes.

Seek the Bottom

This wind's perpetual (despite the gusts
That die as quickly as their kicks are felt),
Provides an undercurrent colder than
You care to pause & feel, moving on.
Between the narrow towers foresting
These blocks the wind was fostering in me
An awful breathlessness, an asthma based
On wonder mixed with wind knocked out, as if
Each gust had kicked me in the guts.
Where pine & cedar used to grow I coughed
To see a wilderness of glass, of loud
And artificial light, the towers foisted,
Wrenched & hoisted, bossing through the dusk,
Of size so prepossessing you might think
They could monopolize your focus, seize
Your eyes as advertisers, Gorgons do,
You frozen to the spot, immoveable,
Your soul afflicted, powerless, drawn back,
Your body heavier than stone, as old
And dense. Perhaps malevolence conceived
These harried straits, not for the benefit
Of anyone who's hurried underneath.
These skyscrapers, so clustered as they are,
Resemble awkward characters with flaws,
Upon their stage, a theatre of brands,
Whose frames reflect a will to overwhelm.
Some want more than a lifetime offers them.
Their monuments, you know, are mutable.
The neighborhood becomes a kind

Of *psychomachia*, externalized,
The inward worry of one mind amid
The millions passing through these straits, Wall Street,
Where only willfulness can stand its ways,
Folks strut or fret according to gyrations,
Upward, downward spiraling, watch out
For vultures hovering. I've heard
Consensus grow: if it's the "ground floor" offer
You've been after & you hope to ride
The crest of yet another bubbling boom
Before it bursts, you seek the bottom first.
The bottoms of my soles will soon wear through
For want of ready money, work that pays
Enough to live. I hold on tight to my
Wool hat, don't want the wind to lift it off
My noggin, warm & snug. It is hand sewn,
This hat, from Donegal, you've seen the kind,
Sole article of quality I own,
A Christmas gift a dozen year ago.
Who sewed it made it fit enough to last.

I Lack Such Scrolls

Were I well off perhaps evasion would
Come easier, perhaps I'd rise above
What is an inconvenience, no more,
To those who can afford to go around,
Not dwell on frailty or hear the tidal
Lowing of the strapped, old radiators
Nullified & cold, invisible
Behind closed doors, walled off, whose breath
In steaming sighs & moans, diminutive,
If they are underneath a roof at all.
I haven't let myself get so upset
In many years, allowed the world to
Burst in on my perceptions, sorrows, griefs
Thought general except to those
Who suffer them, then woefully specific,
Chronic pain, a feeling singled out,
Reduced to tagging vandal, tallying
In litanies what few would care to hear,
The grooves to mark what's never catalogued,
Or having been, has been erased years since.
Folks have their destinations, move along
While I would leave in vain. I have been made
The captive audience before, will be
Again; could not, that frosty night, evade
These voices, bleak as any swollen throat,
Though buckled down, maneuvering; cannot
Ignore the vacancy of eyes that look
So obviously powerless to change,
In need of any change I have to spare,

The mercury in rapid plunge.
This season is supposed to be a glad one,
Gladdest of them all, at least for most.
Gnarled sufferings would frustrate lists
Of loving gratitude. It's hard to hear
Subsistence failing, to see the flesh
So honed, bones weakening. I lack such scrolls
Of grief as bursting sobbed from Kerouac,
Who wept uninterruptedly, left lines
Unraveling as roads that have no end,
Or skin the snake sloughs off: *don't tread on me.*

Old Wonder, New Repairs

The everyday appearance as it strikes
—Wordsworth

Old wonder, new repairs, I saw the cracked-
Archangel spires, jagged, glow like wicks
As dusk set down, the temporal assume
The temple's register, the work of days
Performed within, the ordinary tasks,
Potentially extraordinary where
The raptors, dizzy, spread their wings amid
The zeniths of these shafts, then plunge on rock doves,
Feeding in the street, where growth
Conceals us, our figures in the thick
Of it, low key, at ease though cold. I hope
You will continue on if you're cut out
For compassing the parenthetical.
We'll smell the onions stinking up this town,
The soiled pearls rank with life that swell
Beneath the earth, & pulled & cut as from
A weathered field, reek enough to draw
Your tears; then grilled with peppers, permeate
The intersections, smell like human sweat.
The strike creates a silence out of tune
With nights as usual, no trains that hurl
Rattling along their corridors,
Their bored-out bedrock throats, no tunnel grates
To jar, no ducts to cough, no temple-splitting din
Beleaguering nocturnal wanderers
Tonight, but amplified, low ticks of time.

The strike throws off this density of folks,
Their daily tasks so agonized, prolonged,
Who, disappointed, peer across a bridge
Through moving air & cringe because they're forced
To cross that way on foot, like fugitives,
To walk so far so cold a day, the sun
Already weakened to a coal. I know
Those loads they carry, low wage shifts, each hefty weight.
I shudder at the burdens shouldered over,
Only half-aware till here & now
These umbers numbered so, this blur of folks
Who walk the planks above the cars to reach
The Brooklyn side, who wouldn't show, by train,
But would be subterranean right now.

I Must Digress

Loud carols pour like light & heat from doors
Of shops, car radios, "the blazing *Yule*
Before us... strike the harp & join the chorus."
It's a night to relish colored lights,
To cherish scents of wreaths, for listening
To the vernacular of mysteries,
To look for virtue, mastery of those
Emotions culled when seasons change, the bells
Of carillons go through their repertoire
Of maudlin numbers, overheard, to be
Alone as usual amid so many
Others lost in solitude & not
Dismay, or let some fondness drift too far
Away from here, December in Manhattan,
No remote escapes, but memories
Still islanded down here, still localized
Enough that you could guide another by
Your own account of where things are, or were,
Not just the area, the ownership
In constant flux, but jarring recollections,
Dates & names presumed to have been lost.
I stopped & listened to *So This Is Christmas*
On the way to work, so understated,
Striking inward, chords of sympathy.
I shouldn't let it get to me, so plain
A sentiment, a revolution round
The sun, another set of aspirations
Checked by injuries. Its chant of "War
Is over (if you want it)" leaves me wistful,

Children's voices in the chorus, wondering
What causes war. I heard on lunch-break
Santa Claus Is Coming to Town, The Boss,
Who hollers out the words more than he sings:
"Yuh better watch out, yuh better not cry..." The loss
Is salient since last I sang along
With songs like these, or rattled off old tunes
Beneath my father's roof, the house we shared
Throughout my youth, the family aglow,
Or with that loose & jolly rabblement
That walked the blocks of our old neighborhood
And filled the nights before the holiday
With fa la la la la—*la* la—*la*—*lah*.
Old stations missed when passed, once meant
For rest, such jingles jog my lists & gauge
The distance come since childhood, the breaks
From school down here, as when a sophomore,
I lived *The Catcher in the Rye*, affected
By the meaninglessness shadowing
This life, the mist that covers things, the need
To moan from sudden grief without my sense
Of inner humor dying first, despite
The yuletide cheer. I only pass as one
Who's "fairly Christmassy," although no Scrooge.
I must digress like troubled Holden, form
A remedy, let memory provide,
Prove welcoming to anything that comes,
Allow some freedom to associate,
Let go of any longing for control,
Allow even the cold ingratitude
That greets me gustily to pass, like sleet,
Blow through, as those left panicking with flights
To catch must push & shove along, who will
Not slow their pace, but rather show a wild-
Eyed willingness to fight for any lift,
To be the first in any line, forget
The rest, snatch up another's cab, protest
It benefits the family, admit

One's rudeness then go on, insist, I'm rude
Because nobody will provide for them
But me, & still without the grace of thanks.

The Cold Set In

The cold set in much worse. My feet were dense
With dampness penetrating through my socks.
The wind would not relent, a haunted freeze
Both fatal & indifferent that might
Delight Nathaniel Hawthorne at his desk,
The fire blazing, windows blistering
Like skin with burn of ice without, within
A view of warmth & light, the darkness licked
By tongue of flame, the tunnel of the grate
A storm of drafts, his intellect the focus,
Thinking with some room: I wanted warmth
Of such a nature, & for reasons to be
Mentioned later, ducked into this bar,
The Fraunces Tavern. I've since found that one
Can concentrate effectively down there.
Impatience wanes, you listen in & hear.

Chapter Two

A SENIOR CITIZEN

Scale Unexpected

This tavern stands in contrast to its cavernous
Surroundings, scale unexpected (like
St. Peter's from the 70s, the chapel
Underneath a cantilevered tower,
Lexington & 53rd, the air
Rights sold, the ratio of high & low
Bathetic, for its incongruity).
Amid such depths downtown, this neighborhood
Of banks, you see a pub, commodious,
Beneath the sign of *Queen's Head* in its day,
Bequeathed beyond its Georgian origins
Into this present night. It had its share
Of storied years as Federalist, then gaps
Of scores, decay, revival, now too neat
A reenactment of, or throwback to,
Ye erstwhile days, ye nights of yore, withstands
Your scrutiny, a senior citizen.
Three fires, maybe four, blazed through, razed *Pearl*,
Till half the work of its destruction done,
In longing for those honored days, they tore
It down & built another one, antiqued
In re-creation. Kitsch & camp aside,
It seems to hide in open sight, withdrawn.

Dwelling (Or Its Shell)

In Revolutionary days those soon
Fatigued beneath the royal thumb—the crown
That monarchized, tumescent & obtuse,
A wall of sea three thousand miles between—
While quartering the flanks of soldiery,
Intolerable Acts, would often choose
This well to draw their fill of drafts, from ills
They knew would fly head on for those they chose.
In short, the nation still inchoate it
Was where men cooled their throats for rhetoric,
The leaf bits stuck to lips & teeth, burnt tongues,
Those bossy mouths rumbustious with drams
Of demon water, dozens of them, flint-
Lock marksmen, off half-cocked, & heretics
And bounders, racketeering traffickers.
I see the flash of what authority
Maintains the *status quo*, & those who wish
To overthrow the world now, who'd rush
The citadel, their patience lost, gang up,
Knock down, at liberty to hang themselves,
Together or apart, but one short life
To lose, regrettably, with *Cato's* flourish,
Rectitude of dear old *Cincinnatus*.
It stood at just about the new republic's
Axis ("A republic," said old Ben,
"If you can keep it," fend off wear & tear,
Inevitable top-down-rottenness)
A stone's throw from the island's southeast tip.
Maintained by an endowment I presume,

And housing a museum, it was home
To *War Department* offices, the new
Executive's appointed cabinet
Paid rent in here before the Capitol
Had even been surveyed, malarial,
Before *The Mall* & its museums, all
Those aging bureaus multiplied by ten,
McMillan Plan, the "City Beautiful",
The great marmoreal compartments, frozen
Blocks of grim partitioning, each war
Assigned its own memorial. I think
Of all those countless statesmen, cold, damp looks
Profound, within this work of mortar, trowel,
Brick, the oldest dwelling (or its shell)
Not yet demolished for the sake of higher floors
(*St. Paul's* the sole exception, was, still is);
Of those erratic founders, volatile
Amid the headless mobs, the rare ones groomed
In this long room, who made their voices boom
Above the braying feasts, the fray of guests,
Loud nations needing leaders even louder.

The Point To Stand

It had to be the point to stand before
They flung a bridge across the river's breadth,
Along where J.A. Roebling's foot was crushed,
When ferries breathing wreaths of mist would ply
Its steaming mouth & through the Lower Bay,
The Narrows bottlenecked with sudsy wakes,
And further back, molasses slow to move,
A mid-Atlantic port with room to grow,
Triangulated in a world trade.
You go way back, imagine its beginnings,
Picture taverns & their tables, scenes
As on a canvas of De Hooch, small things
That tell long stories, intricate as days
Of ordinary life, of gatherings
For Netherlandish ale, brewed right there,
A bar to anchor every block with tools
For coping with remoteness, platters full
Of shellfish, zinc for thought & memory,
That copper tang, as if twin ravens settled
On your collar bones & whispered in
Your ears: Manhattan Island is your oyster,
Yes, & *Pearl Street* her opening.

The cellars tossed three thousand broken shells
Out back each night, their oysters broiled, steamed
And pickled, smoked or baked or stewed or fried,
Or on the half-shell, raw, alive. They rose
Till middens, mounds of them, like pearly gates
Enclosed a hidden past, to add to those

Already piled there millennia,
Macadamized when grids were stretched across
Manhattan, intermittently interring
Former worlds, calcium, a slow decay.

Skyward, Engineers

The outcroppings were leveled, swamps reclaimed,
Drained off collects filled in, new ground, the coasts
Increased, encroaching on the river, not
The other way around. The pinch of rent
Gave common pain, amid the ravenous,
The mad for revenues, for quick returns,
Hell-bent beyond the *Mr. Smile* advertised.
They never feared for routs or broils, always
From the ashes rising higher, riding
Sprague & Otis skyward, engineers
The architects, their shelves like quarries, books
Like beams, inherited conglomerates,
The walls in quantity, antiquity
Ransacked, the skeletons of girders cloaked
In glass of cloudy cut, yoked in
By zoning laws, a series of revivals,
Rivalries to show whose tower bosses
Nearest to the sun: *St. Tammany*,
Please tell, *Grand Sachem*, which of these houses, firms,
Embraces heaven closest, has that touch,
And which is gutted from within, a house
Of cards, which scheme of pyramids, a ruse,
Infirm, in need of stimulus, & which
Tall obelisk will be the last of all
These trusts to stand behind its word, by gold,
And which, should Hell exist, would justly dwell,
By God, with all the worst who gained because
They misinformed the world for themselves.

Island Giganticism

Island Giganticism: where species evolve
In ways that leave them vulnerable
As flightless birds watch castaways from shore,
Too long without an adversary, fat,
Too easy prey for pests, once introduced,
As uninvited guests will crash a feast,
Consume what's left of food & booze, or as
A cat will beat the life out of a nest
For play, then lick its bloody paws with an
Artistic patience. *Kudzu* strangles hemlocks,
Leaves them dead. Goodbye to oddities
Extinct as mastodons, the fruits of digs,
The skeletons displayed conjectural.

I Spot a Sketch

Bermuda Rum to sooth a wintry throat,
A *Devil's Island* dram, *rumbullion*,
Those "comfortable waters", like a storm
Contained within a glass, dark history
Distilled from cane, I sniff it deep
And sip a tot of grog to please a tar.
Bermuda: Somers bound for Jamestown struck
Its shore by accident & settled it,
Same year as Hudson entered New York Bay.
Bermuda: where the petrels in the dusk
Would frighten off the wanderer, repel
The faint of heart, their wings around the masts,
As pirates found a haven, privateers,
Confederates. I sniff its painfully
Intense aroma, think of cruelty
Inveterate, of pain gone by, as if
To get in here I walked on unmarked tombs,
Each barrel of molasses made from sweat
Whipped out of harvesters. The char of oak
Is strong because the wood was used to age
A batch of Bourbon, then shipped off to age
The youthful rum, then bottled, shipped again.
I lift my eyes & gaze around a room
That seems preserved in amber, spot a sketch,
A patch of huts, Dutch names: *New Amsterdam*,
And tribal dialects, it is the whole
Of *Len-ap-e-ho-king*, the homeland of
The Delaware, a hacking back to wildness.
That "Bohemian Coast", The *Village* goes

By *Sap-po-kan-i-can*, tobacco crop,
With scarce a trace to hint the present phase,
This populace, but soporific brooks
And ponds by blocks eclipsed, that's hard
To recognize, from "Battery to Bronx",
Changed utterly, the *Bowery* an orchard,
Headstrong Stuyvesant's, "The Rock", retired,
Forced to grant to Doctor Pell his Colony,
The peg-legged old protagonist that pines
Through *Knickerbocker's* tale, one seed
Of Ahab throwing off the habit of his pipe.
There's *Hackensack, Fresh Kills, Bronx Kill,*
The *Kill Van Kull,* & well before they dug
The ship canal, the *Spuyten Duyvil Creek,*
Before its flow was rearranged, amid
The *Inwood marble, Fordham gneiss*
(*Pre-Cambrian,* more than a billion years
Compacted, surfacing), where *Half-Moon* anchored,
Restless dolphin nosing far & wide
For passages that weren't there, mid all
This jewelweed, spicebush, *Cho-rak-a-pok.*
And not far by, *Long Island Sound* spreads wide:
Dubbed *Devil's Belt,* for all the boulders—*Stepping
Stones*—*Old Scratch* once threw across its face,
The narrows where the currents frustrate charts,
Where sloops had no alternative but hope
To reach Manhattan from the Sound, by skillful
Luck to navigate that fevered strait,
Hell Gate, which held the island hostage from
The east, so changeable, so dangerous,
The weather something out of Whistler, boats
Rebuffed for having overlooked the schist
And gneiss, *Cimmerian,* a land of shades
That's harrowing below the buckled surfaces
That whirl through the Gate, once trumpeted
As such, a killer, now sedate, for all
Who drowned against their wills, or felt that scare,
Disaster lists, before they blasted it.

Tangent on "The Slocum"

When the subject was New York the books
Concurred the worst disaster of them all,
Last century, peacetime, for loss
Of human life, was when *The Slocum* burned,
A thousand women, girls, in the flames
Or drowned escaping, no way out for them,
A wound that rippled by degree around
The globe through Dublin's Bloom. Tangentially,
The man for whom the ship was to be named,
A General, had been nicknamed "Slow Come"
At Gettysburg because he vacillated
When he should have charged a ridge, but claimed
Acoustic shade had blocked his orders.
Local folks forgave such lack of hearing
And elected him on top of war-
Time doubts, deserved, folks thought, the honor of
A few things named for him. Bad luck. He bears
A curse that's posthumous, would have
Been better off anonymous, the ship
Synonymous with criminal neglect,
A thousand innocents betrayed, a shifty
Vessel from the start, foreshadowing
Its own demise, its dance with doom, aground
A half a dozen times, collisions, hosts
Of near-disasters till the final one.
And then *Fort Slocum*, derelict, ghost town,
Hart Island, where nobody goes alive,
Except the inmates off *The Rock*, paid half
A buck an hour, ferried by the guards

To reach that *Potter's Field*, dig the rows
That shelve the nameless dead, impoverished,
Nobody claimed, no visitors allowed,
The rusty *Nike* missile silos in
Decay, as empty as the chimneys of
A crumbling graveyard-fort, left islanded
Amid this furious activity,
The jets out of LaGuardia non-stop.
Whereas the scrap & garbage barges head southwest,
The ferry-hearses wake the lower Sound.

The Old Surveyor

Up spiral stairs, you see the long room's boast,
That 4th December toast: the General
George Washington's farewell, his brow one half
As old as time, half dust, half deity,
Like stone that bears a rosy stain, that struck,
Split rock, would flow, sanguineous, a face
Deep-flushed with love & gratitude, it states,
Enough for one last tip of glasses, toast
And old vignette; George Washington, who would
Bedew no face with spittle, drawn to heights of wealth,
Distiller known for what he never did,
That famous hatchet through a cherry tree,
White lies of Mason Weems, who gave the children
Good old honest George; whose obelisk
Was interrupted half way up by war
Between the states, cut off, resumed
At later date, betrays at base a stone
That's different than through its final peak,
Its spike of cast aluminum, in those
Days valued high as gold, so rare it was
(What litters every street in dented cans,
Two dozen empties spilled around a drunk,
A dollar & a quarter worth of them).
This room's a replica of that which held
The ranks of saddened veterans that flanked
Their old surveyor, hard survivor, who
Made risky river crossings. He escaped
The heights of Brooklyn, crossed the East at night,
To fight another day, recovered strength,

Despite his forces dwindling, swollen flanks
Of Howe's; & clove the sullen Delaware,
The sight must be familiar to you
In paint: Emmanuel Leutze, from revolutions,
1848, enthusiastic,
Sought to show the spirit of the risk
Involved, the thrust of *romance, heroism*;
Not, as Rivers, Koch, O'Hara, *romance,*
Heroism... humor: loss of faith
In worn out concepts, darker questioning.
He crossed a stormy Christmas Night, year one
Of Independence, of his men would say,
The crossing's harsh conditions didn't in
The least abate their ardor, no: they seized
The mercenaries by surprise. He played
The fox, maneuvering in dark retreats,
The final victory deferred for years:
George Washington, the venerable pillar,
With a barrel of *Barbados Rum*
Provided for the first inauguration;
Washington, born with his clothes on,
"The American denominator"
There aglow with thermal luster just
Above the hearth. The sight reverberates,
As if a living scene, with latent sound.

Sons of Liberty

The other faces down the bar could be
The *Sons of Liberty*, erecting poles,
Provoking wars with bricks, enframed
By sayings of their fathers, lionized,
Those overthrowing sons, their rhetoric
Thrasonical, about the deeds of war
They honor, not its loutish looting, horrors.
Look into the eyes of those who ratified
The deed, if you can summon them, a print
Or piece of money, any one of these,
The manifold & sundry founders, restless
Sons of Liberty, the rakish, florid,
Vital ones, the usufruct, the new
Ones flowering upon the foundering
Of those beneath the ground, who living seized
The powder house, those rascals crouched
Behind each bush, each blustering decree
More mischievous than first let on, each gaze
Like coal or sap ablaze, at risk, men like
Commodities, as liable to swing.

More Than a Quarter Century Between

No accident that in this bar my Uncle
Comes to mind, a rendezvous between
A sense of fate & what I chanced to meet.
I had been open to what might come up,
And weirdly, found I'd gravitated round
The blocks & wound up close to where my walk
Began, where Broad & Pearl intersect.
Was there I saw a plaque to mark a kind
Of fosse beneath the level of the street,
Brass grate which stirred a fund of memories,
Half-formed, until I walked a little further,
Saw this tavern, said aloud, That door…
Its portal lured me inward, slow, perceptive,
As I entered thought, my Uncle brought
Me through its frame. What year was that? How soon
It seems so late, a decade, two, no, more,
A quarter century comes in between.
Return to roots, well-fixed, relax with room
Enough to muse, to be reminded how
We sat in here & talked one night, these thoughts
As pungent as the myrrh of peaty malt,
Of honey & of heather, snifter's curve
He cradled in his palm to warm it up,
With amber legs extending round the glass,
Like sap, *Drambuie*. Nose & all, I would
Immerse myself in fumes. Now just a sniff,
He'd warn, my face halfway into its bubble,
Not a sip, too hot for your young tongue
To taste as yet. A reminiscence strong
As that, I felt his "presence in his own domain."

On Nightly News I

"Initiation… heretofore unrealized,"
That was Late Fall of 1979,
The cusp of winter, this the month, December…
Anchors numbered off on nightly news
The days of the unfolding hostage crisis,
Fear for those blindfolded diplomats
With rifles hovering about their heads,
The youths of Persia rioting, possessed
The embassy, *Decembrists* of their day,
Their rising irrepressible, & what
One didn't understand seemed most of it.
It was the year, you may recall, The Who
Played Cincinnati: fooled again, the crowd
Stampeded. Folks were crushed, some killed. *The Wall*
Was echoing from FM radios,
Three thousand choruses a day of "we
Don't need no education… need no thought-
Control!" plus hits like "Rock with You" from *Off
The Wall*, "Don't stop till you get enough"
Ubiquitous, atop the charts; about
One year before Mark David Chapman, book
In pocket, flanked the old *Dakota* armed,
And murdered Lennon, cold, outside the door.
This was ten years before the *Berlin Wall*
Came down, before the *Velvet Revolution*;
Havel, fan of *The Velvet Underground*,
Was jailed again, ten years before he'd be
The President. The Soviets would roll
Their tanks that Christmas Day & on the double

Cross into the mountains of Afghanistan.
Those days we were concerned with hockey news.
The *Hartford Civic Center* roof collapsed
The year before beneath the weight of snow
And left *The Whalers* (now defunct) without
A home arena, roaming through the league
They'd hardly joined. But they had Gordie Howe,
Gray haired, to hustle out a final year
Before retirement, *The Hall of Fame.*
The *Islanders* had Bossy, Howe if young
Again, with whom they'd seize the Cup. It was
Two months before we heard the broadcaster
Blurt out, "Do you Believe in miracles?"
Lake Placid fame, The *Miracle on Ice.*

On Nightly News II

It was the year that saw the death of *Nelson*
Rockefeller, grandson of the robber baron;
Yankee catcher Thurman Munson crashed
His plane; of John Wayne, star, more myth than man;
Of Elizabeth Bishop, quiet poet who wrote
The Man-Moth & The Unbeliever, or
At least those were my Uncle's favorites;
Of Allen Tate, the *Fugitive*, while
His fellow *Fugitive*, Robert Penn Warren,
Collected the *Pulitzer Prize*. Odysseus
Elytis was awarded the Nobel.
Mt. Erebus, peak of ice, Antarctica,
Was struck by accident: a jumbo jet
Blindsided it, New Zealand bound, & crashed
Into its frozen wastes, forever lost,
As all on board gave up the ghost, their corpses
Mummified in crevices, unthawed.
Mt. Aetna's throat erupted modestly.
A dam in India collapsed, left thousands
Drowned, while quakes were rocking faulty plates
Throughout Iran, interpreted by some
As ominous for all of us. It was
The year another brother Kennedy
Would run for President. Idi Amin
Would be deposed. A Polish Pope (the first)
Who'd studied for the priesthood underground,
Defied the state, its laws, in favor of
His *calling*, loved the theatre, with ears
For verse, addressed the whole UN, midtown

Manhattan (hadn't faced assassination
Passing through St. Peter's square as yet).
The known petroleum reserves around
The globe had peaked, in retrospect, that spice
Of modern trade, miraculous & cruel,
To rig so many men to sanguine schemes.
A woman, Thatcher (first) became Prime Minister
Across the sea, but news would turn around
The Ulster *Troubles*, skirmishes & bombs.
Mountbatten's boat blew up in *Sligo Bay*,
Beneath *Ben Bulben* tense with violence,
Same day an ambush killed more than a dozen.
News around the globe was terrorism,
Enmities, no peace accord above
The noise was audible, the cameras.
The Grand Mosque, Mecca, even that
Was taken hostage, armed commandoes on
Request to ransom it, same year Iraq
Was seized by coup, a gang of thugs whose boss
And chief abuser was Saddam Hussein,
Supported from these shores, contra Iran,
From here his name synonymous with fog
Of war, wrong rumors, *ignis fatuus*,
Not justice, sanctity, just gasses, death.

On Nightly News III

While *Pioneer 11* passed the rings
Of Saturn, *Voyager* was photographing
Moons of Jupiter, the *Skylab* fell
To pieces, spiraled back to Earth, debris.
The world news could not ignore the *Shah*
And *Ayatollah*, David Rockefeller,
New to me, nor had I read as yet
Of *Kermit* Roosevelt (their grandfathers
Had left them with *responsibilities*,
So hard to bear, so serious they were,
And confident, from robber barons, old
Patroons, a sense they were entitled to
The reins of leadership, the rightful heirs
Of hierarchies: were, in fact, for all
The frightful leverage displayed, the swayed
Elections, rolodex with six degrees
Of networking, well-bound, engrossingly
Fecund with family & family friends).
A caricature of Henry Kissinger
Was sketched in the *New York Review of Books*
In which you only saw his eyes ensconced
In thick old glasses, signature of him,
A spook, like *T. J. Eckleburg*,
Those faceless eyes that brood upon a dump:
"He sees you when you're sleeping, knows when you're
Awake…" America was hated on
The camera, or demonstrations showed
Halfway around the world, nicknamed
Great Satan by the students of Iran.

Folks talked about the power of *cartels*,
The tally at the closing bell in *barrels*,
Shortages, long lines, the empty tankers,
Trucks with empty beds, the days of odd
And even tags, of speculators glad
In it, some bankers with a boom despite
Embargoes, gold gone *through the roof,* the dollar
Low & *bankruptcy* a destiny
The City had but narrowly averted.
Interest rates, inflation, reached fifteen
Percent. Perhaps the news that threatened most
Was from the Susquehanna, partial meltdown,
Three Mile Island, in the "Quaker State,"
In which the tags reminded you, *you have
A friend. The China Syndrome played*
In theatres; *Apocalypse Now.* You heard
Not of the *Falls* but of Niagara's *Love Canal,*
Of toxic "superfunds" or "brown fields."
The Governor of the entire "Empire State,"
Was charismatic, popular, Hugh Carey.

Tangent on the Governor

The Governor? My Grandfather was not
Unlike that man: a politician, lobbyist,
Of stubborn Irish stock, but savvy, quick
Of mind & physically determined,
Rose in Hartford as Hugh Carey did
In Brooklyn; Hartford, where the Morgans
(Real & imagined) were conceived,
The Yankee & the Banker, dead & gone,
The poet of the winter walked his path
To work uninterruptedly, & where
Like Carey Grand Dad mastered that machine
Of local bosses, wards, attended wakes,
Smoked big cigars, wore down his soles,
Would knock on doors, house calls, give rides to polls,
Each thoroughfare his own, became
Well known for his relentlessness, a voice
For oratory, verses. He was liable
To read fine print, the footnotes of a law,
Or write the law himself, the codicils,
His hand in evidence. He represented
Aetna & The Diocese. He shared
A bench at lunch on more than one occasion
With the poet, talked of actuarials,
Perhaps, bonds rates with regulators or,
Their bill just paid, they talked of poetry,
Perhaps *The Rubáiyát*, but none can say.
It's not surprising Carey would've won
The favor of our house, despite the fact
My parents couldn't vote for him, a state

Away, a house in which you'd find
O'Connor's *Last Hurrah* on several shelves,
And jars of campaign pins for Kennedy,
Each brother's run for president. All this
To say years later I would get a chance
To introduce myself to him, the guest
Of honor on St. Patrick's Day, New Haven.
Master of the toast, his Brooklyn voice
Bespoke a kinder spirit than expected,
Full of laughs & witticisms, pointed
Quotes, no gaffes or broken syntax, just
His tested poise. It's still a rarity
To meet someone with such an air of earned
Authority, a posture sure, at ease,
His gestures meant, or seemingly, with force
And grace combined, a sturdy frame behind
Each move, convincing, having spent
A life in politics. It isn't hard
To see the actor Spencer Tracy cast
In Carey's role, the sage professional.
So when at last cigars were handed out
And folks were free to roam the room I shook
His hand & asked him if he knew some Yeats
By heart, as poetry seemed key to him.
"You know, from school, like 'On the pavement's gray'"?
I asked. I was a fool to bother him,
Perhaps, but he was welcoming, more host
Than guest, if slow to turn, exhaling
The smoke from his cigar, his breath with just
A trace of alcohol, the feast: "By heart?
Of course, but not from school; & no, not lines
Like that. You're still young yet..." He weighed the words
Upon his tongue before he said, "We learned:
'Too long a sacrifice can make a stone
Of the heart...'" His memory was moving him,
And then with mischievous solemnity,
He looked me in the eye & shook my hand
Again goodbye, I swear, while he intoned,

"We learned, but never had to be assigned,
To say: 'A terrible beauty is born...'"
Then turned away to greet another guest.

A Child Might Understand

The devil had business on his hand

—Burns

A child might understand in some small way
The symbols waved unnervingly across
The TV screens were worrisome, although
His understanding went no further. My
Bewilderment was great as flags were raised
To rouse those who would say they'd *had enough.*
I didn't know of what or why, since when.
I saw the countless followers of men
That surged like tides against high bars of sand,
Pushed back by Billy-clubs, or beaten flat
In solidarity, the bullied up
Against the bullying, the fearful mobs
Behind some charismatic man in robes
Who treads in austere ways, with graying beard,
Wall-eyed, upon whom you might fear to gaze,
Who uses flaming words to undermine
The thought of peace, pontificating, armed;
Or shaven men in uniforms, who strode
With utter confidence across green lawns
To helicopters, decks of carriers,
Who leaned their hard, oppressive weight
On swagger sticks in contumacious poses,
Clicked & checked the magazines, took aim
With eye through scope, impressed, for kicks,
With aviator shades to ward off glares,
A job to do, divide the flawed terrain,

Projecting odds of victory, to send
The minimum, the maximum expendable;
Or men in Windsor knots & three piece suits
Swept up in verbal rage, indecorous,
Their charge: tomorrow's mutiny,
Disparaging all clarity, the lines
Familiar, the plots redoubtable in all
Their tailored dignity, no word but *hatred*
To describe the *fuel* they lit to launch
What only later one would recognize
As sophistry, the skillful tricks by which
One weakens stronger arguments, turns slick
In favor of the cynical, the few.

Confused Aspiring

My Uncle was an expert on these ways
Folks used persuasion, patiently
Explained how crowds were harboring
Within themselves hot pain, well hurt, resentful
From incitement, longer stories linked
To past injustices, their bandwagons
Were full of smoldering. They formed the rank
And file mobs that rose to douse the flags
And torch the effigies with petrol, fed
The violence I wished to understand,
All heaving heavenward, each having sworn
Beyond the rule of fellow men, beyond
The realm of Caesar, as it were, to realms
Of their deferred deliverance, by grace
Of obligation, risk of castigation, awe,
In hopes of an apocalypse, their own;
Then ostracism, shelling out the cost
Of self-assertion, antinomian
Amid the wood, cut loose to face that wilderness
Of risk alone, confused aspiring,
Surrendering to self-fulfilling prophecies,
The elevator of ethereal
Rewards, from which so few return.
A flood of humans lacking, looking, bursts
The oldest gates, confluences of hunger,
Anger, magnified, the push & shove
For nourishment, their fuming passions
Stricken like a match, luciferous
Against the pitch black situation, no

Relief in sight, benighted, from a life
That—as it was—was full of nothing but
The cruelty of others, suffering.
Why else would they have lost themselves in rage?
For stymied hopes, ignored, the pride they felt
They merited, they seized the instruments
Of destiny by force, another kind
Of boss to feed, another ring to kiss.
From early on one sensed the obvious,
The world was full of obstacles to peace.

Expectant Light

It was the Advent season. Altar boy,
I was the *thurifer* at Mass, who shook
The frankincense & myrrh along the aisle
Of the nave & through the crossing, made
Three sets of triple swings to cense the pews
And altar: *Preparation of the Gifts*,
Inhaled those rich, enchanting trails, shrouds
Of sacred odors, fumes that flowed like thoughts
With holy sway, thoughts fugitive as smoke,
Or clamoring of unseen wings somewhere
Above the arches of the roof, its ribs
And groins of vaulted stone, a finch from eaves
Flown loose, a passage on the soul's way up,
And nearly drifted off to sleep when left
To kneel, dreams high arguments for why
I shouldn't feel light as they, in glass,
The quiet shepherds & their lambs, or call
That pearly brotherhood, the haloed ones,
Who would respond, as later I would love
Chagall, to muse on heights of fertile glass,
The colors cast through motes of dust too small
To catch without that art, disintegrated.
Capitals of pillars, soaring, held
My undivided mind for moments long
Forgotten since. How small I was, how green,
Unfledged, a whelp amid the underwood
Of pews, the ancient boards of which were stained
To shine like wingtip shoes, what rays came through
The windows crazed & cast aslant & glanced

The polished grains of wine-dark cordovan.
I loved to sketch the *Stations of the Cross*
When half in shade, the figures in relief,
The first fall, second, third, the crowded streets,
Some others there to climb that hill's dry skull,
That doleful, darkened day, on which the fate
Of all was acted out as in a theatre
Each spring, dashed off, a Passion play.
Or any other day, set free from school,
I'd draw the cliff of schist that faced my town,
Or burrow in the library so as
To find the books of architecture drawn
For younger minds, & borrow them for months,
Especially Macaulay's *Pyramid*,
Cathedral, City, Underground, & what
Had not been published yet but would be soon,
My final preference, *Unbuilding*, re:
Dismantling the *Empire State*, all done
By pen. I couldn't wait to see them for
Myself, such buildings as he drew, to stand
Beneath their awful height & weight & sketch
Three-point perspectives. Up till then I'd limned
The tallest buildings in expectant light,
Manhattan's leaner towers, far downtown,
From helicopter photographs, would pass
Whole evenings stuck on *70 Pine*,
High & graceful, full of close details
And hard, recalcitrant materials
Subdued as with the lightest touch of force.

It Was Allowed

My Uncle felt he had a role to play
In my development, was up to date,
Aware how much I wanted just to walk
Beneath the architecture, take it in,
Absorb the shock. He soon invited me
To visit him; it was allowed, the old,
Experienced sinner, as it goes, would take
The young beginner through the streets, instruct
His growing mind, & find a spot for dinner.
Mom drove the Parkways down, the *Wilbur Cross*
And wooded *Merritt*, artful bridges, yards
Of old stone walls, half-sunk, & swiftly down
The *Hutchinson*, across the *Triborough Bridge*,
The mainland left behind, the *FDR*
Ahead of us, & let me out at last
On *Maiden Lane*, not far from *Liberty*,
Where I was free to walk about a bit
Before my Uncle would be done with work.
My Uncle, call him Michael, if you like,
Would focus eye for eye unflinchingly,
His handshake firm, his form alive with age,
If unassuming, never first in line,
A spiffy vest, the tie fastidious,
A prescient wit, a fellow striking for
His wakeful mind, a sage New Yorker as
You'll come to find, if you're inclined to walk.

Chapter Three

WE STOOD TOGETHER

A Boy, Cut Loose

I took three steps that afternoon, my own,
Into an open stream of giants, tricky,
Thrown at once beyond my depth, on spires
Gazed, uplifted, towers crystallized as myths,
Their upper windows drenched in waning sun,
The high ones shaken by repeated blasts.
They're built to let the top floors sway
A little in the wind, I'd read. With hands
In pockets, empty, poverty let out
Amid so full a place, I am amazed
To be at intervals exalted—thrilled
To stretch my boundaries, New Haven boy
Who lets it all rush over him, a stomach
Full of butterflies—& dwarfed by hills
Of brick & glass, the layering of works,
And by the traffic at an impasse, jammed,
Both under & above me, huge & savage
Flashes, speckled crowds rebounding from
The bridges & the tunnels, fragmentary,
Leaking light through thick, entangled streets,
Reflecting back the broken beams let through.
As nowhere else on earth it could have been,
That vertical immensity evoked
In me what had a name I didn't know,
Sublimity, demolishing my sense
Of time as myth & math become mish-mashed,
Confused, the city's mysticism, numbers,
Themes, I have since mused, will wind up
Interwoven seamlessly, the past

That had seemed lapsed exhumed, the present made
Composite with these adumbrations of
Those other planes that hide beneath what has
Accumulated, crust a consciousness,
If pointed, can't, won't trust, but must divide,
To strike at what's bequeathed invisibly.
My steps that day were startlingly real,
Solitary: what did I or could
I know or say? There in between, through open
Doors, cut loose, you spot a boy, with eyes
To see & mind to know, without a tongue
To tell his fleeting joy, articulate
His lasting woe, his fears, no words to say,
Unknowable as yet, no end in sight,
To match his sense how worlds move apart
From him, or catch in sounds & images
His wonder how immovable the vastness
Of this lapidary vista is,
Lithe as he goes beneath its glass heights bathed
In shadows, nearly pulled against his will,
Knocked underneath the stream, relieved to hear
His Uncle's holler, recognize that nimble
Figure falling blithely forward down
The block, a fitting sight, adjacent to
The *Chase Manhattan Plaza*, mouth cracked open,
Just about to speak, so that it seemed
That incommunicable mass of folks
Would part before his booming lawyer's voice,
As rock doves vanish hearing owls, "Who?"

As Even Now I See Him

As even now I see him move like sun
Across the sidewalk, teeming crowds
On every side, his specs of tortoise shell
Reflecting back its beams, not snaking through,
No idler's pace. Topmost amid the din,
Like Chaucer's host, a light to counter dusk,
Mercurial, he canters in his over-
Coat across the tense, chaotic inter-
Section, glasses slipping down his nose,
As if a poet in his dotage, wrinkled
Eyelids peeled, crow's feet, looks cajoling
All with wayward sighs, an "Oi?!", "Hello!
What word have you? Make way, by God!" See his
Umbrella brandished like a sword, a Stetson
Set upon his brow he'd tip to nod
And bow as ladies passed before & trod
On by, his gaze unerring, like an elder
Bird of prey, until his neck would twist no more.

Glad To Know

We stood together, thought which way to go
Beneath the shadow of the *Chase*, a wall
Of white. He said that *Maiden Lane* was where
The women used to wash their linens, when
The city was still Dutch, a tiny burg.
Here Uncle started pointing out the sights
He thought worth noting, memorable, that might
Not yet be leveled when I'd guide a nephew
Of my own in years to come. The first was right
In front of us. You will be glad to know,
He said, the architects who built this place
Were active in New Haven, only on
A smaller scale. Here, for instance, is
A tie between a sculptor & an architect,
New York & your home town, the campus there.

Bunschaft is the architect behind
The rare book shrine, a windowless white tomb,
New Haven's *Beinecke*, in which the frail
Volumes are hermetically preserved,
And this, the *Chase* (*The Lever House* as well);
Noguchi is behind this *Sunken Garden*
Set beneath the plaza of the *Chase*,
As well as *Circle, Cube & Pyramid*,
(The Sun, & Chance, & Time, respectively)
Beneath the plaza of the *Beinecke*
(Which *Green Stamps* paid for, unbelievably).
Noguchi said that in the West the theme
Is triumph over gravity, the rocks
Themselves should levitate, or must be made

To seem that way, those big black boulders lifted
From the *Uji River* bottom, from Kyoto
To Manhattan, placed in harmony.
The space is circular, you see, with slopes
Of brick. It's dry today, but in the summer
Fountain water makes them seem to float.
He talked about Noguchi, who had been
Good friends with many other artists known
More commonly, was treated with suspicion
After Pearl Harbor, Japanese-
American. I have since learned he found
Community at *Romany Marie's* café,
Was introduced by Constantine Brancusi,
Sculptor whom my teachers always praised.

Marie? A patron, host, well-known the world
Around, who kept Eugene O'Neill alive,
I've read, by feeding him, let youthful, weird
Buckminster Fuller decorate the walls
With *livingry*, where Joseph Stella also
Ducked for shelter while he worked on what
Would be *New York Interpreted*, the key
Of which, *The Brooklyn Bridge*, was in New Haven,
Hanging in the gallery up there,
A building many loved, by Louis Kahn.

Tangent on the Death of Kahn

Kahn's flowering was late in life & he
Would die in debt, a New York heart attack
(A public death, undraped, as Lowell's was,
A taxi from the airport, neither here
Nor there, but in between, just short).
Kahn's corpse was unidentified for three
Long days, recovered from a filthy station
John, & not the old Penn Station, no,
The new disgusting one. It's difficult
Imagining him there, allusive as
The caryatid photographed amid
The Meadowlands, a travesty to be
So beautiful amid the dump. To think
Of Kahn in no man's land like that, a corpse
Without a tag, would frighten anyone,
A fate so hard, to even hear of it.
Still, harsh as were his life, his ghastly death,
Of little consolation to the man,
He left humanity an afterlife
In architecture, in particular
That gallery I love, first visited
When just a boy with pad & pencil, left
To draw alone, amazed to see a Bosch
Or Bruegel or, as in my adolescence,
Afternoons in winter, I would sit,
Not draw, & let myself go suffering
Through Rothko's hues of grief, those panes
That open up like windows on his blood,
Induced a state so bleak it was sublime.

At The Crossroads

The *Sunken Garden*, yes, *Four Trees*, as well,
That shapely set of trunks, near shapelessness,
The other sculpture underneath the *Chase*,
By Dubuffet, so memorable, had been
Commissioned by the Rockefeller brothers,
Sons who from their mother learned just how
And what to buy, with taste, to cultivate
A certain eye, warned off of controversy
By their father's conflict with Rivera.
David was the youngest one, the banker,
Fed the press reluctantly that year,
Because he'd used substantial leverage
To intervene to save the Shah, on his
Behalf the President gave in, to grant
A visa to the *Mayo Clinic*, sparked,
Or helped to spark, along with Kissinger,
No doubt, it seems from here, the hostage crisis.
Fault's not found in one man but the few,
Whose plausible deniability
Is hard for folks to nail under law.
Old loyalties are inextricable
From royalties, you understand, the laws
They've spun eviscerating other laws
More just to those with little say. The types
Of policies they have preserved remain
To keep the few well-heeled & reward
The years of service, propped on lower backs
Repressively, on people's fears, black-ops,
The willingness to use the rack & stretch

Resistance to its breaking point, defeat.
Good news about the hostages was long
In coming, as most folks recall. A year
Would pass before a skilled Algerian
Negotiated freedom for each captive
(Ransomed for what price, one speculates,
What promises aside from what was said?)
Soon welcomed home with tickertape along
The *Heroes' Canyon*, glad to have escaped.

Manhattan Company

And *Chase Manhattan*, what of that, beneath
Whose massive tower we were circumspect?
From *The Manhattan Company*, way back,
From Aaron Burr, competing with, against,
The Hamilton monopoly. Few think
Of Burr as hero on Manhattan through
The *War for Independence*, or know how
With members of the foot-guard he repelled
The Red Coats from New Haven, more like Arnold
In the memory, a turncoat but
Acquitted. Burr, the legend goes, would be
George Washington's *Iago*, held a grudge
When service wasn't recognized, despite
The fact he'd been at *Valley Forge*, that lamp
So dim when everything was darkest. Years
To come the Chief Executive would go
So far as block the archives, Burr's access
Denied, to keep him back, prevent a book
About the war, with him as author, one
That wouldn't be so kind to Washington,
Or so one tale reads. The libeled Burr!
Who formed the first political machine
Complete with wards & bosses, tenements
He leased to citizens fresh off the boats
To push his chosen votes, the Irish fresh
Across, their faces dirty, tongues on fire,
Thick with sweetest brogues, a flowering
Of folks to flood the polls, the populace
To lift his plank, defeat his enemies,

Put Tammany to use, but never joined.
He died a speculator, as he lived,
Whose leases couldn't lift him out of debt,
Divorced a final time, a second stroke
(The first at Monmouth, day of bloody rout).
The *Chase*? The Rockefeller Bank. They merge
And merge again, you can't keep up with them,
In constant flux, acquisitively fixed.
We took our time & sauntered off at half
The pace I would've walked, with nonchalance,
Up William Street, up William stepped to John.
And so he guided me past crannied spots
I would have missed if left to find my way
Alone, spots vanished now, as if beneath
The streets a parallel necropolis
Was flourishing as he imagined it,
As if the walls were flowering with tales.
For instance *Golden Hill*, no more a hill,
Round Cliff & John, where fields of wheat were sewn
By Dutch, & bricks were thrown at Red Coats once
By *Sons of Liberty*. No evidence
Remains to naked eye. It was within
A block or so of there that Tyler's *Contrast*
Played the sold out *John Street Theatre*
To vigorous applause, which Washington,
In all his manliness, is said to have
Enjoyed enough to bare his ivory teeth,
Not wooden as one learns, but elephant
Or hippopotamus, like scrimshaw, carved from tusks,
If I'm not simply being gullible.

Older Scales

Down Nassau then, we passed an imitation
Florentine Palazzo, banking's days
Of glory, mounds of gold beneath, a pile
Heavier than any floor could hold,
On bedrock heaped, a trust, a sacred crypt,
Eclipsed from gold of sun by wall of stone,
The fundamental element of shine.
I was absorbed in all I saw, & he
Enjoyed the newness through my eyes, a boy
In awe, as we proceeded onward, past
The corridors of Pine & Cedar, names
To summon forests full of them, plucked up,
Cut down; & like a burr I stuck to him
As we retraced our steps, digressed to points
Northwest, as pilgrim spirits, pioneers
Of the interior, so I could see
The old *St. Peter's* on St. Peter's Street,
Then Church Street to *St. Paul's*, the oldest house
Continuously erect, in use, downtown,
Survivor of the fires of the past,
Of mica schist with brownstone quoins,
A portico & tower topped with what
Was called the *Lantern of Diogenes*,
Choragic Monument, design employed
For Civil War Memorials, well-known.
George Washington maintained a pew,
Pierre L'Enfant left evidence of glory,
Naming two who figure in its story.
A third & final church awaited us,

Down Broadway South to Rector Street, the head
Of Wall, to contemplate the stony yard
Of *Trinity*, the oldest yard around,
The spire once the tallest mark downtown,
Now dwarfed by all its neighbors, banks.
We paused to make a note of older scales,
Precincts of the common spirit prior
To the elevator, heavenward
Their exaltations focused on designs
Unalterable, their altars blessed with gifts,
The sextants ringing in the hours for
The benefit of laborers whose patience
Was their real skill, their will to be exact.

We Saw the Grave

And then we saw the grave of Hamilton.
Most follow Hamilton, for whom some folks
Assume I'm named (I'm not), while few
Admire Burr, hear shots from Weehawken,
The weakening of Burr, ironically,
By death of Hamilton, with whom a party
Wounded in the *Whiskey Rebellion* died,
Burr's shot its fatal blow, a Quincy Adams
Grim reminder of a past that's gone;
And further off, hear falls of Paterson,
The mills of industry that were to be,
Passaic River, flowing with a voice
Like William Carlos Williams, soothing roll
Through his environs, younger than his years.
I also think of Gore Vidal, his cutting
Narrative, a kind of *Mugwump*'s, not
Unlike *Democracy*, the novel, days
Of out & out corruption, brawling, pillar-
Biters trumpeting betrayals, treasons,
Irony beyond their ken. It's clear
That Old Vidal knew *Knickerbocker*'s book,
Revived as if by séance, bachelor
Of searching wit, Ik Marvel-like but for
The rigor of a devil that he brought
To bear on what he sought, symbolic heir
Of Brooks & Henry Adams, Ezra Pound,
Repining in Rapallo, toughened, gray,
American, an avatar of Irving,
Breaks for smokes in *William Cullen Bryant Park*.

Navel of the World

Nothing in the latest advice from Wall Street
Inclines me to give up my holdings in patient grief

—Robert Frost

We pivoted & tacked, crossed currents, turned
Down Wall, the *Irving Trust* at 1, a kind
Of counterpoint to Trinity; & reached
That famous intersection, Wall & Broad,
Possessive axis of securities.
We saw the bronze of Washington, the work
Of Ward, John Quincy Adams Ward, who cast
The *Shakespeare* statue up in *Central Park*.

The actor *Edwin Booth*, the "Hundred Nights Hamlet",
Raised the funds performing with his brother,
John Wilkes Booth, who would assassinate
The president within a year. The play
They staged was obviously *Julius Caesar*.
Edwin Booth? He entertained a crowd beneath
The ground, in *Mammoth Cave*, Kentucky,
Just as P.T. Barnum's Jenny Lind
(That's why *Booth's Amphitheatre*). *Booth's Theatre*
Went into bankruptcy, but from his house
At Gramercy he fed the stage. John Sargent's *Booth*
(I've only seen a print) still hangs in there.
He passed down books, props, costumes, sets,
To theatre posterity, as any
Player knows (I cannot say I've seen,
Unfortunately, his statue at the center
Of that private park. It's gated, locked

To passersby, nor do I have key).

We saw the Doric Porch, the Pantheon
And Parthenon epitomized, a dome,
The columns white as tusks or birch bark scrolls,
Bleak rock, well-hewn, the architect named Town,
Whose bones are buried in New Haven, Uncle said,
Behind a large Egyptian pylon-gate.
He said when Town was eight years old,
His father having died, he moved
Into his Uncle's house, & fetched him books.
Collecting books on architecture kept
Him occupied, until his shelves could count
Eleven thousand volumes, open to
A younger set to browse like elephants
Or thieves, those up & coming youths who saw
Within the promise of an architect,
The generations swallowed in those stacks.
He taught the good ones how to learn themselves.
Town's Lattice Truss was his design, from which
He made his fortune (easy way to build
A covered bridge, like those upstate, such as
The *Eaglesville* that spans the *Battenkill*,
The planks diagonally fixed, the truss
He patented before the *Burr*, that truss
Whose fretwork often spanned the *Susquehanna*).

We paused to look around that spinning hub
Of antic bustle, point of leverage,
Where Archimedes might have moved the earth,
Remuneratively. And he explained
In measured words how many of these folks
We saw down here would call this corner
Intersection navel of the world,
Caesar's world, as it were, his temple
To the temporal, with all revolving
Doors & vestibules & steps to haunted halls.
So much is centered here, the trading pits,
The firms of high (& low) finance, the giants

Of the indices who've leveraged
Themselves to reach a perch of dominance,
However short their stay, however long
Their wizardry (pay no attention to that man
Behind the curtain, Dorothy)
Achieves returns, eyes fixed to screens, their thoughts
On fluctuations in the currency,
The distant offspring of some numismatic cult
With Mercury for patron, faces struck
To mark the leadership in trust, amid
Those shielded by checkbooks, wielding
Their cash heroically, whose contribution
Is to hedge the world's bets for fees,
That incrementally (if well-invested,
Just as often not) may raise what will
At first appear to be a lasting stash,
A leverage that's envied. Still, no wand
In hand, no power to prevent stampeding
When the panic spreads across the herd,
A cyclical unraveling, that fall
Like Humpty Dumpty's, valuations found
Absurd, the fundamental worth's erased.
Here wailing was heard on blackest days,
The so called navel of the earth, the center,
Never holds, leaves pummeled shares, a crash.
As houses fell & cash went up in smoke,
Men plummeted, some saw no choice but jump.

Tangent on Morgan

23 Wall, old *House of Morgan*, propped
The markets up, his seat on the Exchange
New York's *Cathedra Petri*, liturgy
Of vatic traders heard between
The opening & closing bells. A bomb
Went off outside, the Great War just behind,
But that was after J.P. Morgan's death.
J. Pierpont Morgan, master of the house
That bore his name, a lover of the big
Cigars, who puffed as much tobacco as
Ulysses S. Grant & Samuel L. Clemens
Combined, economies of scale, floated
Bonds across the sea, a man of funds
For storming through, self-conscious though, his nose
Diseased, turned violent when photographed.
He gutted weaker trusts, went through the fittest,
Taught the world how to *Morganize*,
And christened *US Steel*, controlled
The girders & the nails, all of it,
The beams & ties, monopolized the stuff
Till *Bethlehem* spun off, some of his own.
His preference was *Clubs of Hercules*,
Havana, by the crate. Folks look to him despite
A century between, his absence felt,
A longing for his final word, for one
Of regnant certainty, an integrated man,
The only one who could've locked the doors & forced
Accords by opening the books, an eye
For cracks in the accounting, kept his perch

In an apartment looking down on all
The neighborhood, a bird of prey,
His floor up there, the thirty first,
At *14 Wall*, his view beneath
The seven story pyramid that marks
Its pinnacle. The financier without
A peer, Leviathan, collected books
As well as livelihoods & companies.
If you should seek a trove of rarities,
His shelves will leave you overwhelmed, include
Blake's *Job*, *A Christmas Carol*, Dickens'
Manuscript of it, & many others
Far too numerous to list, a host
Of *incunabula*, along with swaths
Of *scholia*, first drafts, the cribbed & crossed
Out verses in their cradles, stricken lines
With scribblings, revised, the palimpsests,
The scrolls & velum codices,
Embellishments, rich dyes, depictions of
The scenes from scriptures, holy lore, motifs
So crucial to two thousand years of art.

One hundred years beyond the panic he
Averted, narrowly, a renovation
Lets some rays of light down through the roof.
The architect, Piano, said
That poetry would serve as metaphor
For what he wanted to achieve, to add,
Enhance that fund of prior skills displayed
(McKim, of Pennsylvania Station fame),
Made new, inviting. Walk up Madison
Avenue through Murray Hill, when you're
Not rushed to reach Grand Central Terminal.
J. Pierpont Morgan died in Rome, in bed,
Asleep, a suite inside the *Grand Hotel*,
Not far from plaques for Shelley, Keats,
The *Spanish Steps*, commiserable man
Of money, the invulnerable master,

Mortal. When his coffin passed down Wall
They struck the flags, the market closed two hours.
His grave's in Hartford, *Cedar Hill*, up north.

Such Offices

Meanwhile I was looking up the tapered
Limestone trunk—topmost, as if a mast
Or obelisk, or snowcapped peak,
But gothic in its ornament, *New Style*—
Of the tower at *70 Pine*, its tip
Encased in glass, an eagle's nest from which,
Clear days, Long Island Sound & all
Five boroughs come within a glance,
A tower far too tall to comprehend,
Unutterably high, me openmouthed,
Imagining myself a double looking down
On sidewalk deep below: what would I have
To do to occupy such offices?
Another loomed: *20 Exchange Place*,
By *Cross & Cross*, the architects, who were
Behind the *Union Trust* at Elm & Church,
The one adjacent to *The Green*,
New Haven; "Federal Vocabulary",
"Colonial Revivalism," the cupola
A counterpoint to the United Church,
New Haven scale, height about a third
Of any tower with a name down here
(My father worked on the eleventh floor,
From which the pinnacle emerged, topped off
With little room, trap door hatched through its floor,
A little dome from which the view seemed higher
Than it is to me today. We rode
The elevators when attendants sat
In uniform on wooden stools to ask

Which floor you had in mind, accompanied
You up & down. The elevator stopped
At the eleventh floor. There were three sets
Of spiral stairs on top of that to reach
The cupola & visibility).
They also built the old *GE* above
The dome of *St. Bartholomew*, same brick
Of salmon color, tall & beautiful,
Congruity, clear ratio of high
And low, of crowning shaft & nave in scale.
Then Uncle said, look up, a pyramid
Should be its pinnacle, as *14 Wall*,
But then the Crash: they had to cut it off,
The financing fell through, just like
11 Madison Avenue, what would
Have been a hundred stories, equal to
The *Empire State*, just stopped.
You see it looming there, Gargantuan,
Not unlike Bruegel's *Babel*, incomplete,
Its base too wide, no shaft or capital,
Beside St. Mark's (its *Met Life* replica),
Old Venice scales zoned to boast "New York".

Bossy Sculptures

Beneath that tower, 20 Exchange, at Broad,
We saw the bossy men of stone carved five
To seven flights above the street, like monks
Prepared to fight, anointed knights.
They are like gargoyles in function,
Altered for the world of the markets,
Haughty gazes warding off no Devil
But defying folks' uncertainty,
Strong-based, they offer permanence to catch
A client's lagging confidence. Look up,
It almost looks like they are pissing down
On us, he laughed, they're readying to spray!
There used to be a bridge right here, across
The Broad Canal, *Rialto* of the Dutch,
Before the buttonwood, the stock exchange
That formed beneath its limbs. Down Broad
To Beaver (trappers, after all, the first
Economy, a boom in furs, top hats
Of pelt or felt unpopular these days,
Manhattan for the most part hatless now)
Then Whitehall, off to Bowling Green, we saw
A fountain there where George the Third once placed
A statue of himself, erected as
Reminder who was boss, deliverer
From seven years of war (*The French & Indian*),
That boss despised, despite his Roman pose,
"Equestrian", the stoical Aurelius
Upon his horse, a lapidary scrawl
Beneath his majesty's hyperbole,

Before the people tore it down, the mob
Had had enough, young Jonathan grew fierce,
Took arms against a power seas between,
To write the Devil's Scripture over him
And sing the chorus, "No more Kings!", awaken,
Rise, throw off that old servility
Forever, free to fall: his pedestal
Creates a throne remote from common men.
Let the world be taxed, & let it be
Upon our backs, but let us vote this for
Ourselves, no more imperial music.
He'd been contemptuous, repugnant to
The good of all, considered them seduced
Into revolt by rogues & their attorneys,
The ingratitude of commoners,
Promiscuous, a mob. But see his jowl,
Decadent & loose, his lazy scowl
Fattened, tyrant's gut distended, bilious
And rude his haughty attitude, there cast
In regnant form, embodied on the green,
A kingdom fed on poorer backs, by tax—
Until the mob with grievances up to
Their necks, their patience lost, stormed through
The citadel & toppled him, the king
Beheaded (as at Whitehall, London, years
Before, the regicides & Charles the First,
Van Dyck's heroic, mounted subject) marched
The head in effigy through half-lit streets,
Pure mayhem, like a tar-&-feathering,
Burlesque, the noble horse & torso of
The king absconded by the foundries, melted
Down to bullets, sorely needed lead,
The flintlock musket muzzles cold for lack
Of ammunition, not for lack of will
To ram the powder home & squeeze one off.

A Tangent On Nast & St. Nicholas

Later generations often found a way
To overthrow a Boss non-violently.
One tested way: the satirist was hard
At work to sketch the vulture *Tweed*. You've seen
The fat distended dollar signs corrupt
Beyond what one would think was possible.
It was that doubting Thomas "Nasty" Nast,
His devil of a will to salt a wound,
To pick a scar, expose & kill the tumor,
Once it's diagnosed, who brought the Boss
Of Tammany, a fugitive, before
The law, so long delayed, that officer
So insolent, as with entitlements
Convinced the courts can't touch his bigger lies,
The petty bully siphoning the dole,
A hall the cost of which would overrun
All but the boldest of imaginations,
Gifting cronies with the phoniest
Of grafted jobs, to show his gratitude,
The finest of plutocracies for sale.
With pen & ink Nast told a graphic tale,
Scolded with the power of his art.
You could've been illiterate, & gotten it.
I'd say the real nastiness of Nast
Was that he showed himself a Nativist
Reactionary, hostile to the flood
Of famished immigrants, said "huddled masses,"
Woe of Babylon, those saying Mass
The worst, saw hassles in their muddled Latin,

Superstitions, poverty, beyond
The pale, crocodiles lurking in
The murky local Ganges, "jack-tars, teagues,"
John Adams would have said, the refugees,
Their cradles not filled right, but rocking forth
With infants of the poor, no room for them.
And yet old Nast was capable of grace
Despite the teeth he showed to folks who would
In time conceive, deliver me into
Another century, alive & curious
(I have inherited the earth).
Nast must be credited, the prior charge
Dismissed, the record struck, because
Of mitigating art: he left a gift
For all, the winter's Nick we know, that sly
Old elf of poetry, but sketched,
The *Santa Claus, St. Nicholas,* up north,
Victorious, avuncular as Irving.
Department stores were next, the holiday
Was launched in visuals, new customs fixed
As old, antiqued newfangledness, till soon
Nativities, the manger & the crib
St. Francis filled, his cave of loving gifts
(Who in St. Nicholas, the Church, would turn
The Scripture's pages to a single passage
One, then two, & then three times, & by
That sortilege became convinced the time
Had come for him to be a mendicant)
Would serve as window props for shop displays,
Commercial saturation, till a child
Was forgivable for mixing Nick
The saint with Christ (or *Old* Nick for that matter)
And for the fear he would be weighed, found wanting,
Punishments his dole & not rewards,
The father, most severe, & not the son,
To dwell upon the thought *He sees me when
I'm sleeping, knows when I'm awake:* I must
Be good, or lumps of coal will fill my stocking,

Scorn not gifts. In school I memorized
Those lines by Moore (or just attributed
To him, whose name I thought was "Clemency")
Which we, along with Luke & Matthew, saved
To read before the fire once a year
While nestled in on Christmas Eve, "In hopes
Saint Nick would soon be there"; or, "Behold,
There came wise men"; or shepherds quaking, saying,
"Now," to one another, "Let us go… & see."

Chapter Four

AMID THE EXCAVATIONS

We Had To Loiter

Stone to Broad, our feet were tired now,
So that when we had reached the lower row
Of older landmarks, *Captain Kidd was here*,
Where Pearl opens up the vanished slip
Round Coenties Alley, where the water gates
Once kept the port, & we beheld a school
Of archeologists, conjecturing
What lay below, my Uncle said let's stop
And loiter here a while, watch them use
Their trowels. They were testing squares with screens
Of mesh, a fellowship on hands & knees
Like penitents, or like the children in
A sandbox, playing on all fours, ordained
To lift the veil of the intervening years,
To peel off the layers, husk & rind,
To find the past intact, the fruits in trust,
Emancipate the ghosts that cling to things,
The rust & char, the proof of fires singed
Into the sediment, to realize
The building of their dreams. They had their work
Cut out for them, a loam of heaps to sift,
Thin, veiled plies. Perhaps their staff would strike
A trace of blood, rocks split, their scholarship,
So accurate, would lead them to unearth
A flattened stem of wrinkled time complete
With tulip petals, or they'd be the first
To touch some distant strain too long unheard,
Too quiet otherwise, confined to dark,
Amid the rubble & debris of Dutch

And English hospitality, cut deep
Into a theatre of crumbling walls,
As *Chumley's* chimney, bound to up & fall,
And spill a history in broken brick
As thick as leaves around a sycamore.

No Stone Unturned, Had They the Time

The residues would have to be wiped off
And scrutinized, carved out, the clues scooped up
And marked as evidence, though frayed. They said
They'd leave no stone unturned, had they the time
To take their time but they had not: their time
Was limited, two months amid the moles
To have those items out of hiding, reach
The darker, deeper part. My Uncle, proud
But almost sad, looked down into the heart
Of what had been: remains beneath the lid
Of piled earth that offers only hints.
He beamed with envy at the way they seized
The history & followed through, their cause
A closer look, a keener sense of how
The founders lived. He wished to stay & watch
Them zero in & shovel out that pit
Of clay, that clutch of ash, of shells & fill,
The imperscriptible, considered trash
By most, to reach, all hoped, the *City Tavern*,
Walls & all, recover more than just
Bleak rocks, but reach its cornerstones: to will
Back into being what's invisible
Because of time, redeem by reassembling,
What left no ruins to the naked eye,
The tables where they coped with settlement,
The topers with their sour ale washing down
Each bowl of chowder, oyster stew, the first
Manhattan City Hall, the Dutch *Stadt Huys*,
A bar & inn & then the Hall, long gone.

Or thereabouts, perhaps they'd excavate
The *Lovelace* Tavern, artifacts you would
Expect to date, the broken hands of clocks,
The oil lamps & candles, soot, the draff
Of firkins cracked, the work of carpenters,
Discarded planks, reduced to splinters, tacks
And nails, keys from locksmiths, anything
At all, some oyster shells, could be concealing
A rarity: the least of it was deemed
Invaluable & called for their precise,
Exacting scrutiny, a thankless task
For them to undertake, so few mud-puddle
Blossoms sprouting out of it, some flakes
Of evidence for all that laboring.

Possible Without Collapsing

The first of many taverns, inns, the place
Was shoddily constructed, verged close
Upon the wharves, a brewery attached.
The posts that shored it up were piled near
High tide as possible without collapsing
Into it, along the slip, canal.
Now years come in between, so that you see
The alley's yards from where the flood tide runs,
Manhattan having mushroomed round its shores
With fill when shares on Wall have boomed. And then
A cavity, half vacant lot, a wrinkle
In the folds of time, a mix of gravel,
Oyster shells & shards of bottlenecks,
Of *Piels*, brothers once from Brooklyn,
Reingold, Ballantine, the three ringed ale,
And *Ruppert's Knickerbocker Beer*, defunct
(The beer that paid for Babe & for "The House
That *Ruppert* Built," the Bronx, already fixed
And renovated, soon to be demolished,
New one rising in the neighborhood).
Left fallow through delays, the 70's,
While financing went through, this level spot
Was slated as the future site of an
Enormous granite Global Bank. For them
To excavate was inconvenient
When time had come to build. The talks broke down,
But the developers were forced to cease,
Desist & let this fellowship commence
Their lofty, humbling work, to ply & sift

Around for those mute walls before the bank's
New tower rose into the sky, black windows
Covered it for good, a bargain struck
Where structures raised to last are razed before
You even notice they've been lost, & just
Beneath their surfaces? Some swear of ghosts,
At least, possess a sense there's more, unfound.

Village Scale

My Uncle's flat on Perry Street, where I
Would have a fold-out cot that night, a brownstone,
Village scale, open shutters, shimmers
Through my memory, a den of tomes,
His mind a mansion crammed inside its rooms.
Low stacks would serve as coffee tables.
Feeble towers of law reviews
Hung scaffolded neck-high along the hall,
And two refrigerators, one for food,
The other full of books, a makeshift shelf.
So many pearls of wisdom seemed to be
Clasped tightly in the spines & shells
Of folios. He raked the cinders, kindled
Fatwood, added oak & watched the fire
Roar to life. He often cracked a large
Encyclopedia to check a fact,
But acted more enthusiastically
About the mysticism packed in even
Ordinary books, potentially.
He spoke of the occult great readers past
And present look to cultivate, who seek
To touch a random leaf of text & deem
A knotty code by *stichomancy*. Once
He just picked up a random book & flipped
With eyes closed through the pages, placed
His finger on a word & focused there.
The book was London's *People of the Abyss*.
He claimed it was as much about Manhattan
As ostensibly on London,

Issue of a soul once washed up on
The rocks round City Hall, stuck down amid
The lower strata. There were countless volumes,
Knickerbocker's, Putnam's Magazines,
The *East Village Other*, edges yellow,
Thrown in ample boxes with *The Voice*.
I saw his reading played a sacred role,
As he would rock in his old Hitchcock chair,
One book after another, arms unscrolled,
The lamp with slightly tilted shade
Illuminating manuscripts of notes
He scrawled while reading with his pen.

What Underlay the World

Now pile your dust upon the quick and dead
Till of this flat a mountain you have made

—Laertes, *Hamlet*

I came to understand what underlay
The world for this old bachelor was books,
"A means to the imagination's grace,"
Each spiritual fact, great stacks of them,
Like vines on trellises grown thick with fruit,
Well-pruned, or like the trellises themselves,
Brick walls, or pilings driven into rock,
Or cornerstones, each binding structural,
Each page a beam, each line a bolt, each word
With loads to bear so that the heights might soar.

The whole, in sum, looms greater than its parts,
The planks of which soon sag with all the weight
Of thumb-smudged paperbacks, their edges smoothed
To roundedness, the bearded volumes thick
With charms to sooth the hurt of things, to mend
What falls apart through intervening years.
He seemed to reach from shore to shore by dint
Of will, by reading through, enchanting form,
His little flat a great immensity,
At home in any one of them, as snug
As any oyster in his chair, or out
Amid the neighborhood, a saunterer,
As if a navigator monk, cut loose
In coracle, the spirit's distances

Immense, the body's limits nearer home.
I see him thrive in some *scriptorium*,
Some cloister where the clerics read all day
And night, his own *Iona*, not yet sacked,
Much brighter for the darkness bordering,
The murdering that hems him in. I hear
His rites of reading, like old liturgies
To bear his emphasis, renewable,
Enacted in the heart, condolences
To one who with the words he fought through, fraught
With energies he hardly understood,
Returned a little smarter, journeyman
No more, unraveling the lesser things
He wrought for worthier ascents, from all
This suffering a love that's filial,
What focuses a life of soulfulness,
The hours spent lamenting him no waste.

Another Death To Brave

And soon enough, foreseeably, you've lost
Another one you love, another death
To brave, more ashes thrust into your face,
More thoughts about the walks, forgotten nights,
More dust to walk upon, to think of ghosts
Of the departed, real as a dream
From which you had no wish to wake, in which
They breathe & blink again. I'm vexed at his
Brown study now, as Ransom wrote, a poem
Present in a half a dozen books,
Anthologies, he gave as Christmas gifts.
He left a stack of ancient magazines,
A trunk he tagged for me before he died,
A simple note attached to it, unseen
At first, left hidden in the flat, that said
"These items are for Ham, to be preserved."
He made his living room, entire place,
Hospitable to poetry, to keep
A kind of purity at heart, in mind.
The rest, as Hazlitt quotes from *As You Like It*,
Is mere oblivion, *a dead letter.*

Dear Old Lady

Astir with questionings, surrounded by
The evidence of history a cold
December evening, the sky grown dark
Amid the archeologists at work,
I asked about the family past. Not once,
But many times my Grandmother had said,
You are an *Underhill*, & solemnly
Instructed me how much it meant to her;
You must remember this. On Christmas Eve
She'd rub my hand & whisper tales, dub
New York *New Amsterdam*, soon handed down
Her trunk of books to me, a tree with coat
Of arms, her theme lost cause, as works of Scott,
Although I think that she preferred O'Henry
(Who would sink into his cups at *Pete's*,
On *Irving Place*: the quiet lodger, author
Of *The Gift of the Magi*, which concludes
That those who give the gifts, they are
The wisest ones, they are the *magic* ones,
Their holidays are made of gratitude).
I hear my Uncle laugh, repeating it,
An *Underhill*... an *Underhill*?! Alright,
I understand. But be forewarned, although
Some genealogies are well & good,
In that they shouldn't be discarded, I
Regard the most of them like some disease
You have inherited a weakness for
It's best to keep yourself from catching, heel
Of Achilles, kryptonite, you choose

Your metaphor, third rail, flowing, flown,
The past that's dead, or killed, like neighborhoods,
Or family wealth. And yet without some sense
Of roots & branches all is lost. She gave
Herself to dreams that would enrich the hurt
Of poverty, a fate she hadn't wanted, forced
Upon her. So she sees him as a star
That's set apart from all the rest, that shows
She can be proud of who she is, forgives
The deeds of violence, remote from her,
Through him a link to heroism, link
For you to share with her, your ancestor.
But she can't hear his gripes & oaths, his Dutch
Accent, too vulgar for her ears, can't see
His acts without the film of ancestry
Distorting them. I hear his devilishly
Acid tongue, see thickened skin, his mouth
A dirty soldier's. Helena De Hooch,
His first wife: she was Dutch. The painter's name
But unrelated, I would guess. His sister:
Petronella; daughter, Deborah; & by
His second wife, Elizabeth, it's true,
You are a long descendent from that line
Of Abrahams & Isaacs, Quakers fond
Of tags from Scripture, farmers in their day.

To Understand Her Origins

At the flat he would've fixed his lamp
On documents to answer. There & then
His smile beamed on me with mixture of
A gentle mockery & high esteem,
Avuncular. He said that Royall Tyler
Poked his share of fun at some Manhattan
Pedigrees, *John Richard Robert Jacob*
Isaac Abraham Cornelius Van Dumpling,
Made up for that purpose, digs & jibes,
A rise out of an audience composed
Of Jonathans & Ichabods & just
A few who'd seen a play or two before.
Most thought they'd stepped into *The School for Scandal.*
But for your grandmother, you'll have to try
To understand her origins, from Rye
And Amawalk, Mamaroneck, White Plains,
Ten generations undisturbed before
The crash caught up with them, their world collapsed.
She knew the consequences of great loss
Because her youth was full of wealth but when
She turned fifteen her father blew the last
Of her inheritance, that Fall when Wall
Was just another name for destitute.
She had no dowry to rely on, found
A naval officer, your father's dad,
And insofar as it was possible
For wives of officers, she settled down.
Something there was that wanted Wall Street
Down... her father too, but they went on

And she would dream like a Virginian
Of lost causes, costs she just could not afford,
And never bought a single share of stock,
Just bonds & bank accounts insured for all
Their worth: she was severely risk averse.

A World in Another World's Defeat

Her Underhill, I know in retrospect,
As with his portrait in the genealogy,
Was fraudulent, but something wished for,
Noteworthy hearsay.

One of his descendents, CEO
Of *US Steel*, went to London, full
Of cash & gullibility to find
A portrait of John Underhill. He found
A gallery to look for one, to make
His dream come true: a portrait to be hung
With pride of ancestry, his Cavalier.
The agent was inventive, slick enough
To satisfy a need. He fooled him well,
With something feasible. The Captain had
Returned to London, 1638
To print his book, *News from America*,
About the Pequot War; same year, same town,
Van Dyck was hard at work on portraits of
The English. I would add, New Haven had
Its founding April of that year. So if
You knew that Underhill was over there
You might believe it was the real thing,
What was in fact a copy of an old
Van Dyck: the year was accurate enough,
Believable, to lead the patron on,
Although the real thing is hanging in
Brazil, the "MAS-P", São Paulo.
Grandma's Underhill was consolation,
Centered her. The Genealogical Society

Concedes their portrait is a fake,
But Grandma died before that revelation.
She would open up the tree & say,
Just look, you see, you have his nose. I'd say
It was a dream that came from poetry
Like Quaker Greenleaf Whittier's, who held
The heretic in high esteem, a man
Who like his ancestors had paid the price
For conscience, said of Underhill he was
As one *To whom the freedom of the earth*
Was given, alone with the infinite purity.
He was the penitent who smote the heathen.
In *The Algerine Captive*, Royall Tyler's
Narrator, Updike Underhill, descends
From Captain John, a loyal fighter wronged.
Some readers thought he was sincere & traced
Their roots to fiction, one *Benoni*
Underhill, made up by Tyler, claimed
By old New Hampshire trees. They missed
The spirit of his irony, the art
Of Swift & Sterne & Fielding: the way
They chose to disabuse the common use
Of history, turned upside down,
Revealing, as they amused as well, the worst
Excesses of their age, where no excuse
Is worthy to forgive the folly so
Enthusiastically embraced. They would
Provide relief from heroism, such
Tall talk as walks about in brass & flaunts
Its ugliest atrocities, remove
The masks of those who'd oversimplify, repeat,
The advertiser's drift of history,
Contrive the proof as from whole cloth, till folks
Are cloaked in shawls of ignorance, lose sight
Of who they were, or where they're going, or
Decide the truth is worthless anyway,
Whatever it's supposed to be, to whom.
His character's remote from what she would

Have tolerated privately but he
Was of Elizabethan parentage,
Held famous for his ardent liberty,
"The perfect man." You have inherited
A world in another world's defeat,
My Uncle said, a myth that's been prolonged,
Captain Underhill, your kinsman.

Yours to Build On

And so while still amid the excavations,
Tune of taxis husky through the cold
And gusty canyons, crackling puddles frozen
Underfoot, the dusky weight of stone
Uplifted nearly infinite, the heights
Turned overcast, blank slate above
Our divagations, Uncle took my hand,
Said never mind these crowds, let's climb
This tavern's steps, though underage, I think
You're old enough, tonight, they know me here.
I'll tell you all about New Amsterdam,
Old John. You know, he said, a bomb went off
In here four years ago, but nobody
Was ever nicked for it. They say a cannonball
Burst through, beginning of the Revolution.
He'd prefer a rocking chair, he said,
To keep a swaying rhythm, even rhyme
If time should lead his thoughts that way, recall
The rhymes of history. I often drift
Through stacks, my boy, through files full of halos,
Warped with gleaming round the founders' names,
But their contemporaries were at odds,
So you will learn you too must constantly
Revise your understanding: they
Were men not gods, so I advise you read
With catholicity, be skeptical,
Avoid the ease with which you see the folks
Convinced to hotly take one side & fight
On its behalf, the whole beyond the grasp

Of comprehension, closed against opposing
Points of view before they're even made.
I'm going to tell you what I tallied out
Of litigations, long unknown to most,
The dust on them grown thick, with nobody
To guide me but myself, a labyrinth
Of twists that form a pattern, opening
To hosts of bibliographies. If I
Disclose a fact or two along the way,
It's yours to build on in the years to come.

A nephew passes down his uncle's gift,
Another uncle, to another nephew, lines
That span the rift of years & go between.

Chapter Five

REGARD HIS DAY

The Devil's Territories

Look back on him: he looks forward to you,
Your bleak, half-savage source. Regard his day.
"The inessential houses melt away."
This was before the dawn of office towers,
Before the barges filled with garbage bound
For *Fresh Kills* jammed the harbor, that great dump
Had mounted to a monumental hill
Of man; before the island known for years
As *Little Oyster Island* grew by fill to be
The *Isle of Tears*, or *Ellis Island*, as
It is remembered, gate through which
The multitudes would pass, their whispering
The sound of gratitude; before *The Rock*
Of *Rikers* was the world's largest penal island,
Noisy with the agonies of young
Incarceration, bad narcotics, junk
Withdrawal, locked too close for peace;
Prior to *Indian Point*, reactor cores;
Three centuries before immense peacetime
Explosions, watched by thousands, cleared the rocks
At *Hell Gate*; prior to the *Hell Gate Bridge*,
A youth, from which the view is high & wide,
You'll see while riding on the Amtrak home;
Before the *European Starling* was released
In *Central Park*, in honor of the Bard,
From eighty birds two hundred million,
The *Quaker Parrot* (or *Monk Parakeet*)
Became acclimatized; before the Park
Itself was but a gleam in Olmstead's eye,

Was made to seem exemplary of that
Which thrived before, cleared off, not quite
A virgin land as some insist, but no
Doubt maidenly, wild, difficult
To cross, once called by old Divines
The *Devil's Territories*, where the devil,
Irritated, lurked behind the thickets,
Bushes, trunks, before irradiated
By the Lord, Long Island Sound a woody
Theatre of drumlins, eskers, cliffs
And till, striations in the schist,
Deep grooves, a kettle lake (that's *Ronkonkoma*,
Steeped in lore, the local ghost a girl's
Death) & terminal moraine. Regard
A grassy stage of plots forgotten, cluttered
Boulders, large erratics crawling glaciers
Dropped while thawing, coils sloughed, great walls
Of flowing slurry, gradually withdrawing
Altogether: Glover's Rock, Split Rock
And Judge's Cave (where *Regicides* would hide
From soldiers), left behind in random places,
Bordering on squelchy marshes, swamps,
Fens, bogs, low tides that squirm, life now
Extinct, the ossified remains, loose shells,
The open spaces, meadows full of streams.
The lapsing pulse of flowing water wells
Upon the shallows' rocks & splashes them,
The tide once high retreats to low again,
The screams you hear aren't human screams but hawks.
Before the Library, the Croton Reservoir,
Its grave Egyptian walls of forty four
And a half feet tall (you could parade
Around the rim, spot *Trinity* downtown),
Demolished for the coming stacks of books,
Before the likes of Lenox & of Astor,
Prior even to the farm that grew before
The Reservoir, astonishing to view:
A new world lay before those few who'd crossed.

Worlds Thawed

Imagine shallows sting with jellyfish
(That's not too difficult), the currents charge
With bloated sturgeon, runs of salmon, schools
Of mackerel, the shad & winter flounder,
Bass & blues; the mermaid's hair in strands
Along each estuary shore.
The forests fill with voices of the wrens
And vireos, their floors a host of shrews
And voles, with beds of acorns, worlds thawed
When mild wind reverses off the littoral.
The rivers figure as the arteries
And veins of one great giant, nothing to
Impede their flow but for the dwarfish beaver
Lodge & dam, still free of mills.
The blizzards tear the branches off,
Form driftage for the beavers, thunderstorms
And lightning strikes, the listless branches float
Down stream in spring, until the silted mouth
Collects them, like the sediment in bars
And jutting necks, with prints from ibises,
No taint of mercury, where cormorants
Weigh down the boughs like overfed
Philosophers, the shoreline caked with mussels,
Periwinkles, channeled whelks
In which you hear an echo of the Sound.
Mergansers fly across the sky, mute swans,
Oldsquaws, least terns & ruddy ducks,
Where *Onrust*, first of European ships
Entirely made of New World wood,

Was christened by the skipper Block who sailed
Restlessly, uncharted estuaries, noted
Iron in the traprock cliffs that makes
Them red to naked eye, described the faces
Where the thermals waft the harriers
Half way heavenward. Peruse a world
Lost to us, once crowded out, laid flat,
Rebuilt. Look back again: list catalogues
Of zones of green to log, burn, warp, saw, whittle
Down to scrimshaw pawns. Touch oak bark, peel
Birch, the wire & the paper birch
To roll for scrolls. Stir pitch until you've got
A feel for it. Take a stroll, relax,
Divide your shares beneath the buttonwood,
Leave offerings beneath the shady yew,
The revenants alive as evergreens
With limbs that whistle in the winter wind.
If you could smell so many types of pine!
Not yet the countless coffins split & knocked
Together, planks of former trunks folks lay
In plots, the millions that fill the yards.
Swing willow boughs, sniff foxy vines, cut elms
For switches crack as whips of hide. Sketch ash,
Catch locusts, loaf beneath a world of shades.
Hear bull frogs leap about the lily pads,
Snatch clouds of flies with nothing but their tongues.
Sniff skunks in great abundance. Ospreys guard
The windy shore, their hovering remarkable,
Where golden eagles hunt alone, descend
From nests in topmost crags, their nobler claims,
Where *Hobomock* is known to hibernate.

Examples Must Be Made

It was too much for Dutch & English settlers'
Breathless eyes to ken, take in, in awe—
Connecticut & Paumanok, the germ
Of what you see now merged, concrete downtown,
Not streets but alleys, crooked villages—
Imaginations incommensurate
With what they saw, without retreating from
Those Devil's woods into the Jealousy
Of God. Ingratitude from traders, soon
Much worse, their dwindling lot in broken talks,
Coerced, their boundaries all crossed like streets,
With streets, decorum intersected, scars
And escalations, sanctity debased,
In essence "Stuck between a rock & a hard place,"
The *Lenape*, or *Delaware*, were crossed
Beyond all dignity, then massacred;
Until the *Siwanoy*, among the rest,
Chief Wampage their foremost warrior,
Struck back. *Pavonia & Hackensack*
Attacked, De Vries convinced to leave again,
Anne Hutchinson & family were dead.

Chief Wampage became *Anne Hook*: he killed
Her but he kept her red-haired daughter,
Stained *Split Rock* with blood, erratic boulder,
Bronx, struck fear into the populace,
Who fled into the fort. The *Siwanoy*
Would raise that daughter far away
From the New England Way, so that her fate
Was called captivity, a pearl lost,

And since not ransomed soon enough, they found
The little girl hacked backed to the wild,
Changed for good, preferred the *Siwanoy*.

So burghers in their frightened meetings pressed
For heavy business, wanted bloody beatings,
Mercenary arms. Examples must
Be made of insolence, they said—there would
Be no mistake. They pressed their testy head,
No burgess of the forest but a tool
Of trade, to hire someone capable,
For they were traffickers, not warriors,
Those Dutch, so turned to someone clutch, a kind
Of slugger to pinch hit: John Underhill.

Useful With His Skill in Arms

Captain Underhill, tall fellow, man
Of errors, tales just as tall, prodigious
In his lustiness, an Englishman
In exile, veteran of brutal wars
Amid the Low Countries, another of
That stubborn crew of errant so-called Saints
(Or fools) who crossed into New England with
The Great Migration, eager, militant
To build by fire, musket, prophecy,
To quote the text, to level pike & apt
Pericope, prepare for the *parousia*...
He found himself accused of heresy.

He had to flee, too controversial,
To find a strand to call his own beyond
The rule of orthodoxy. So it was
With Mrs. Hutchinson, agreed, one mind
Between the ministers & magistrates,
That she should be cast forth into the woods
Of Mephistophilis, a stirrer up
Of strife, knocked home with snickering when she
Was struck by fatal blow, the chief elect
Of them convinced beyond all doubt she had
Deserved her fate, her punishment at hands
Of savages, mere analogues to their
Interpreters, the *Siwanoy* contrived
As figurations of an intervening
Holy wrath, unwitting messengers,
Forget about the deeds of Testy Kieft,
The obvious, the plain & brutal facts.

As she was driven off, so was the Captain,
Tried & sent away, but useful with
His skill in arms, he came to aid the Dutch,
To rectify that blood spill, eye to eye.
For news of Captain Underhill, who was
The tallest, blackest messenger of war,
Like wildfire, or disease, had spread
Throughout the colonies, that he had burned
The Mystic *Pequots* dead, their village ash,
As Melville said, extinct as Medes (though,
Of course, that wasn't true: they'd resurrect).

And thus for reputation one of flesh,
And fierce, they granted him excessive use
Of force, a proven quantity, to see
Their errand run without remorse;
They wished to entertain no second thoughts,
So bought his services… The price was dear,
Perhaps, compared to what they teach it cost
The Dutch to buy Manhattan from their hosts.

He Sped Up History

The *Wappingers* would serve for sacrifice.
Below a moon as bright as day, blue lawn
Of icy snow, the very dead
Of winter, Captain Underhill,
Refractory, erratic, torched his foes,
Their windy corpses black, all filthy air,
Before an awkward squad of drafted men
Recruited for that harsh occasion. Skin
And blood, the hair, the smoke would sicken them.
The Captain, like a demon, hectored all
Those greenhorns dwarfed & cowering.
Stentorian his holler, red the color
Of his spirit, power rolling onward
Unappeased, in him an army rose
To lead the rest to arms, his opposition
Crimson, melting down a trail of wrath,
Triumphant marches, wakes. With Sachem heads
On spikes, their flesh in shreds, mere paling
Forms, he sped up history,
Returned, awarded property,
Where *Trinity* stands now, its yard
Of stones, the head of Wall. But records show
That he would sell it soon; no doubt old John
Had found the place too much in town
(Left all behind for Flushing, Oyster Bay).

That Dig We Saw

(St. Patrick's Day 1644)

And so that dig we saw, the *City Tavern*,
Following the victory, or rout,
Was Bruegel-lively: there they all unite
Within a hazy hovel, warm & quaint
And boozy, smoky from tobacco, flush
With Dutch & English folks from up through *Hell Gate*,
Round the Sound & down the Lower Bay,
Bronx Kill to *Kill Van Kull*, from *Fairfield* down
To the *Isle of Meadows*, *Pavonia*,
And old *Communipaw* of fable.
Underhill, beam in his eye, with ale
Enthused, one set of knuckles bruised but resting
On his belted hip, the other lifting
High a frothy tankard, hat tipped back
As if King David painted brashly by
The clever Dutch who quartered him,
Impatient for Bathsheba, nodding by
The stove, about to lurch at any moment,
Rash & unpredictable, too pissed,
A contumacious man, commenced a prized
Example of his etiquette, commenced
A drunken incident. Suppose you're there
To watch the soldier swell with excess pride.
In leather boots he points his spraying boasts
At one or other cozy burgher's face,
Like ancient Pistol brags the world's but
His oyster, shucked by sword. He's slurping down
Two dozen, blows pipe fumes from boozy lips

And harps on all his bloodshed, ceaselessly.
You hear the kind of blusterer who rages
On & on, about advantage of
Surprise, a devil spouting out of spiteful
Springs both praise & blame, the former
For the Dutch initiative, the wisdom
In their strategy, the fact that they
Had nerve enough to hire him, the latter
For the Dutch timidity with arms,
That they had need of him at all, the traffickers.
And thus worse than a fireplace in which
The flue's still blocked, the lout blew smoke all night,
A gloating churl, his scurrility
Without restraint, a cocky, slurring, drunken rant
Concocted of the rudest words poured out,
Like no carouser could, his exhalations
Spirited, until at last he settled on
This one demand: that those inside the bar
Should raise a toast to honor him, who loomed
In tested arms (tall talk): "Your savior, New Netherlands!"

Sword Drawn, Lord Knows

Everardus Bogardus, the minister
On hand, his wife with him, one Opdyke there
As well, ignored the blasphemous toast, ate on.
The Captain's noggin blossomed like a tumor,
Focus reddened angrily, flared nerves.
He yelled out they should join his toast
And all that captive audience agreed
Except for Opdyke & Bogardus, who
Provoked by their refusal an attack
From Underhill, who loathed the ministers
And let loose tides of slander, hurled oaths:
You're countermanded by a stronger man!
I have experience, you cowards. Enough!
He was at liberty to have it out
With them right here, that ruffian! Sword drawn,
Lord knows, he wouldn't be insulted by
A Dutchman, or a minister, not both;
And so he pounced, a wolf on huddled lambs.
The din was no dull roar, but strength of chest
In it, with throat of burly colic gusts,
I mean this was a tongue-lashing, a host
Of caustic threats, those soft mixed colonists
Appalled, with dropping jaws, left dumb, while he
Grew angrier, his right hand man, as drunk
As he was, Baxter, offering his share,
Their drummer boy bombastically in time
With them—drunken momentum, shattering
With sharpened arms the mugs of clay, dispersing
Many guest who hadn't gone. The folks

Agreed: he was an ugly customer.
The hostess pleaded, Captain Van Der Hull!
Oh won't you let us be in peace, just take
Your ale & go! Don't slash the drapes, don't dash
The cups, don't ruin us… But no. Too drunk,
Bewitched & ravening, induced to fight,
His scabbard in his left hand, sword held firmly
In his right, he swore aloud, you would
Cast stones? Beware, clear out of here, I strike
At random now. These hands, provoked, break necks.
The guards were sent for as the uproar grew,
And came, but did no good, just met with his
Same insolence & laughter, threats to go
Ahead with bets & watch me kill you after.
Beery losels, slumberous bores! What kicks
To watch the smoking burghers squirm! It seems
Ignoble, but to Underhill? The kind
Of fit for which old surly, braggart John,
The hired soldier, could be proud, to mock
The dainty traffickers & spit at will.

Grace Abounded

He must've loved to glower overbearingly
Upon the stiffened minister & frighten
Off his chastened wife, as if *Old Scratch*
Himself. He stuffed his pipe full of another
Guest's tobacco, knocked the plates & bottles
Off the broken shelves. Bogardus was
Insistent, call the Testy Kieft, Director,
Have him clear away the backslider.
Most having fled, too few of them were left
To watch, or later testify, & yet
At least one witness swore John Underhill
Rebuked Bogardus, hollered, Kieft, that fine,
Just let him come & see. I'd rather share
Some words with him than with the rest of all
You devils put together. Nothing left
To break, & nobody remaining in
His broken wake, the hostess swept the shards
And shells in piles, dumped them in the back.
He spoiled every meeting, blasted through
That fellowship. The folks would leave for home
Exhaling a tale of a vandal's crime.
Though grievances were filed, sources some
Historian might cite, I won't, he failed
To appear in court. In brief, he flew
To *Paumanok*, profound belief in his
Own faculties unshaken, stretched
And basked in sun. Old soldier, reprobate,
Fierce, gentle magistrate; an arsonist,
A profligate, a rounder; hale granted

Use of force, the elements so mixed
In him it's no surprise he struck assurance
Grace abounded in his case because
He smoked rank weed, tobacco, prayed
Into his pipe, a farce, before the rank
And file orthodox of Boston blubbered
Forth a fraudulent retraction, frothy
With conniving, having travestied
Their Holy Sabbath Day. He locked the door
To pray in privacy—as in Vermeer's
The Soldier & the Laughing Girl—with one
Whose spouse was seven months at sea,
The gossipers suspicious on her steps,
No choice but stray again from colony
To colony, a hired man. And though
I do not know the selling price, he sold,
I've read, the *House of Hope* near Hartford twice,
A place the river's course has eaten up.

He scoffed down what he found of ale,
Clams & eggs, & never fail, wed
Into the family of his nemesis,
A younger wife in later life, a maid
Of higher station from a Quaker congregation,
Softened by another generation,
Rover flanked by tribes of children, wound
Up fattened as a monk, at last moved on
To Locust Valley, weighty friend
Of the *Matinecocks*, from whom he gained
His deed, his yard, his *Killingworth*,
A shout from shore on Oyster Bay.

His heritage, the Sound, a theatre
Of war, stretched wide before, he yawned
Then swore out *God* & slipped away.
For this he may be crowned *American*.

***

A note to add: in 1907,
The same year as the Wall Street Panic Morgan
Wrestled into order, Underhill's
Descendents raised a goodly sum to build,
Beside a cedar tree at Oyster Bay,
An obelisk of granite (*Hallowell*)
Surmounted by, in bronze, a ball to which
An eagle clings, an emblem of the line
From Warwickshire that crossed the sea & made
America their claim, commemorating
Captain John, the founder of that line.
To mark the dedication, Roosevelt,
The President from *Sagamore*, next door,
Came by & used the family to stump
For "equal opportunity", as they
Used him for notoriety. Among
The guests was Francis Townsend Underhill,
Who'd ridden up the *San Juan Hill* abreast
Of Roosevelt, achieved some dwindling fame
In Montecito, California,
For horseflesh, yachts, & landscape architecture.
Roosevelt, behind the *Great White Fleet*,
Soft speech, big stick, announced: I have no use
Whatever for the man the best of whom
Is underground. There is an Underhill
In every walk of life; I wouldn't be
Here otherwise, my fellow Long Islanders.

Chapter Six

THEY'RE HOLDING UP
THE HOLIDAY

A darker, ruder pilgrimage…
An exhausting & uncertain effort
For something more substantial, elevated

—Whittier

My Uncle Seemed to Follow Me That Night

All this was a long time ago. Perry Street,
Where Uncle had his flat, has not changed much.
But others occupy it now, so that
I rarely veer that way because I know
I'll feel hollowness, a smoldering
Despair: since he's been gone it's just a street,
Or worse, a haunted area, what hits
Me hard an absence felt as hurt, what won't
Return to how it was, forever lost.
And yet my Uncle, never mind the flat,
Is felt as presence too, that's unconfined,
And as I summon up that evening
The talks broke down, the strike began, I'd swear
My Uncle followed me around that day,
I had discovered something old but new
To me, a world shared between us though
Such matters are irrational. I think
It's not too far a stretch to say that he
Was an unhealed wound I have redressed
For his avuncular inheritance
To be passed down, as if he patiently
Expected my return; as if hence forth
Into posterity in debt to him
And not to him alone, I know I must
Invest myself in him, return the favor,
Saunter further on without a guide
Like him again, his gift to send me off,
Once gone, from opening matured, his line
Of argument a bit over my head,

Enticing me to learn his terms, pursue
Some line of inquiry, somewhere
His ways of learning pointed towards,
Unsettling, the end of which was through
Another labyrinth unknowable
Without the willingness to suffer means
Of change, pass through & reappear, as if
The ordinary never seemed so strange.
I have continued to swerve off, step free,
On other nights since then, avoided rushing
Home to meet my poverty, again,
Refused to go unthinkingly, would not
Knock under it, the stream of market crowds,
That great deluge, but halt, as grinding gears,
And watch folks fight for first in line, regard
Profusion not for me to share, the flash
Of outward forms impelled impatiently,
But cut across the currents, as that night
I waded through assembled forces, murky
Stretches far beneath the mammoth banks,
Benighted stone, went plunging on with no
Expression, waiting for a sign, until
I saw a brass plaque marking out the ex-
Cavations we discovered on our walk,
If wanting to, a night that I could not
Forget, December 1979,
Where Broad & Pearl open up, the old
Canal & slip, the navel of the early
Settlement, a venerable spot
To pause & contemplate the history.

They never found the *City Tavern*'s walls,
For all the tribulations they endured,
Though you can see the *Lovelace Tavern* there,
Beneath the grates, perhaps hear whispering,
The old brown porter poured to quench
A thirsty grief, tobacco smoke puffed out,
The regulars who would be called to arms,
In disbelief: mere fragments of a wall

Do not a tavern make. I tread this dust
And think of all the wares once hawked round here,
The stock & surplus narrowed down to this.
Some artifacts from ordinary life
Were found intact, some pewter spoons they used
To stir their tea, mature patinas, pipes
And onion bottles; but beneath a slab
They struck a deeper fosse, a well, where souls
Around more than two hundred & fifty years
Ago would draw up water, clean, cool, pure,
With yeast to scatter, start another brew.
Cold shade, too dark: no sunlight ever hits
But fleetingly, aslant, beneath that bossy
Granite global banking dragon lodged
So heavily above that layered spot
Of old Manhattan times, that cut
Stone Street in half. I crossed the street & stepped
Into the tavern where these memories
Unfolded doubly, modified, where I
Commenced, reluctantly at first, in notes,
To draw up prints in lines still tentative,
Because I felt a duty was incumbent:
Raise him up, remember once again.

Allure of Holidays

Recovered Uncles would be jolly

—Dylan Thomas

A wreath hung from the glass & wooden door,
Thud shut, the lintel tricked with mistletoe,
The pearly berries swaddled in its leaves.
A sudden heat & I was in the hall.
For holidays they cut a tree, decked richly,
Ornaments from bough to bough, up to
The star, topmost. By glow of voices guided,
Murmuring, I crouched beside the hearth,
The *Balthazars* & *Melchiors* of wine
Matured & racked in caves, Gargantuan
Those bubbly gifts, repressed by cork & wire,
Curve of glass reflecting back the flames,
Mid evidence of routs & ravening.
It's quieter than recent memory
The servers must admit. I think of him,
That night, his furrowed, lapidary brow;
One glance: he takes you in his confidence.
He would convey his gratitude for this
As well, a hint more than coincidence
He can't confirm, a man of subtle mark
To comprehend your growing mind, a kind
Of friendly ghost to mend the dark. I wish
We could have aged together. No such stroke
Of luck, his death was sudden: I won't let
Him dwindle now, will go so far as say
He's with me still & I'm the boulder tough

To budge which mentions him, that says
To all who hear, his dignity abides
In me, revered, well loved, beyond
The shadow of a doubt a soul upright,
My star that dwells within, but far apart,
Maintained, my origins aligned with his
By threaded twists in spirit, sturdy knots,
As hearing him recite from Hamlet by
The mantle Christmas Eve, that swath of text
About the "bird of dawning": wholesome…
Hallowed… gracious is that time." But then
The carols from the radio break in,
Derail this, a marathon of such
Familiar tunes it's hard to tune them out,
Especially when one has lyrics close
To the emotion of this lonesomeness,
As when tears surface & escape against
Your wishes, listening, evoked by one
That sings of "cloven skies" through which we see
And hear "the angels hurl". The weary world,
Glad below, so long fatigued, enjoys
Relief from suffering, songs lodged
"On hovering wing", descending as
The angels bend above the world's "Babel sounds"
(That otherwise surround) to do their singing.
Here are words that captivate, I would
Have liked to write myself, so jot them down:
"A man at war with man hears not
The love song which they bring. O hush
The noise ye men of strife & hear
The angels sing… Beneath life's crushing load…
With painful steps & slow… the weary road…
The ever-circling years… the day
Foretold… send back the song which now
The angels sing." I will remember it.

I'm on the Fence

The way the shadows lengthen, night grows long,
I think of Sloan's *McSorley's*, "Ash Can School",
Raw onions, dusky mugs of ale, pale
Cast of thought, the wary ones, the bar
Thinned out, stares sapped & withering: are these
The sons of revolution or of pleasure?
Nearer to their voices I can hear
They are disputants, cracking wise, a pair
Of wakeful brains, their jawing tongue in cheek.
In fact they are negotiators, eyes
On *Seven News*, closed-captioning, the bar
Their hiding place, their voices loud enough
That soon they have provoked the bartender
To speak his views, philosophize, address
Their transit strike. I hear his sigh let out
Like pressure from a radiator, steam.
He frowns, as if to say, I learned the things
I know, but no degree was earned, just lines
Of worry, wincing over bitterness
Of hops, the bitterest the most preferred.
He speaks at last: You want free sense—the strike?!
Three days at tops, no more. You disagree?
I know, I know, you would prefer to hear
"Good News," read headlines coined for all,
"The Union Wins", a victory deferred
For long enough. I love you guys, I do,
But there won't be a revolution—not
Tonight, tomorrow night, at all. The strike
Will draw its final card, cave in, both sides

Agree to settle for a very little gain.
Or brace yourself, you might get fleeced again,
Nobody knows, not even you. Would be
A stroke of luck beyond what anyone
Expects for you to win. Should hell freeze over,
Your demands get met, but here & now,
The best scenario? The board will shell
Out just enough to buy some extra pints
Of beer, a token bone gets thrown your way,
But not enough to please your wives, your kids,
The kind of benefits, the coverage
You have in mind. There's nothing to be done.
You want the mine but wind up with the shaft.
I wouldn't want to spend my shifts beneath
The ground, hell no, I sympathize:
The life expectancy is low, the cost
Of living high, the daylight minimum,
The air obscure, no windows, fireplace
Or door like mine. I can't complain. And now
They've banned tobacco smoke in bars: cleaned up
The inner air so I breathe easier,
But underground? It's brutal, just too dark.
Some folks cry foul, call it lawlessness,
For you to strike this week. I understand
You throw around the power that you've got,
But folks have bitched & moaned a lot.
"They're holding up the holiday," I hear,
Bold move, unfair to everyone, the poor
Especially. I'm on the fence, would fall
In line with you because I know you need
To live, but draw the line between us on
The choice of when you force your hand. Just look
At me: I serve, I'm honest, but collect
No bonuses except for tips I hope
Grow fat as geese this time of year, each bit
Contributing, a little extra all
Around, but now, who knows? Ingratitude?
I won't be splurging on the latest toys.

The taps slow down & then don't flow at all.
Tonight, the next few nights, I will enjoy
No "seasonal munificence", *last call*
Won't be that late; I'll have to pay a cab.

But Linger On

But linger on until we close, he said
To them, & turned & said to me, or when
You choose to go, just range around
The darkened passages, the architecture
Vacant, nobody but you, the windows
Blank, the towers lodging only bits of light.
The world turns to glass despite its weight.
And he elaborates: You see, without
The bridge & tunnel crowd? Sheer vacancy.
Manhattan folks may dump on them, but here
We are, like Sabbath night on Wall, just look
Around & listen closely, silence, weird,
The elevators open, grounded in their lobbies,
Empty, soundless as the grave.
I hear the groan of cruelty released
A little while, weight above put down.
He says, You'd roll before each door a stone,
Tonight, tomorrow night, I swear, no one
Would care, just sober talk like this between
The longest silences, & even Broadway,
Still. So many cross to reach this island:
Their imaginations make the place.
Fact is these thoughts are not original.
As you walk down the steps & out, you'll know
I'm right, spot buildings, streets, but not a soul.
It's something beautiful, or rare at least…

Down in the Heart

I stepped outside to roll a cigarette
Before returning for another rum, more talk,
Enjoyed the silence, spirits fled from zones
Held sacred, streets like naves & crossings. I
Should have agreed with him, it's beautiful
And rare down here: this vacancy would be
Our poverty if solitude & quiet
Were no more than that, mere emptiness
Instead of layered worlds, flowering,
If only one should quickly look below,
And longer, but I kept my mouth shut tight,
No Shelley cited from my buttoned lips.
This kind of cold is purifying, for
A while. Think, this is New York, downtown,
And nobody is here. It's *serious*,
Engravable, between two dispensations,
Winter's start, the solstice round the corner,
Shortest day & longest night, the light
To wax from here that was diminishing
Since June, the zodiac in cusp, just days
Until the holiday, a strike, & there
I am, one full of love, down in the heart,
And wondering how these old streets that cross
To make the navel of a world—point
Around which countless fortunes turn, roulettes
Revolving, canyons jammed in such profusion
In between the bells—could bate & dwindle,
Wind up void of folks, a deadening,
A cornered solitude, a few stray honks,

Funereal, no neighborhood to mourn.
This spot was thronged, now kithless, lorn of pulse,
It is the emptiest of theatres.
I know it has been gutted many times,
Will be again, torn down, a lodge of ghosts.
The lamps against the dampness of the ice
Give off a glow, as in the lines we learned
When very young about St. Nicholas,
The moon, the breast of newly fallen snow,
The midday luster, objects below, with nothing
To dread, as when these chimneys aren't only
Kindling light & heat, with logs to knock
For sparkling harbingers, but changed into
Those thresholds children glow & dream beneath,
About to hatch great troves of gifts, such gifts,
So magical, as opening they grow
To see, wide eyes in awe that won't quite last.
Although aware no belly (bowl of jelly)
Ever fit through any stout old hearth,
No larger star appears with pearly glow
This time of year, I can't help think of lines
Forgotten once before: were I to hear
Somebody say, "come see the oxen kneel,"
I'd want to go with him "into the gloom."

Another Voice

The emptiness surrounding me is like
A silent gift that's well-received. I hear
Another voice invade that void, return
To me, twice told: Shrewd lad, go, rise without
The help of all those kin, enough of this
Reflecting back on disinheritance,
The nightmares others dreamed & lived. Arise
From yards of stone, the past & all its lists
Of cruelties, ancestral weight of wrongs.
Go celebrate long nights of solitude,
Revere yourself, though balked & dumb, your thoughts
On what's to come. Remember blood was spilled,
But leave behind the boasts of ancestry.
I know, as Uncle, even Underhill,
Though retrograde, confronted, stared down at
Some point: "the I & the Abyss"—as if
A turkey vulture circles overhead,
Foreshadowing what's dead—
Must come to pass but can't be shepherded.
This is the poverty of one who would
Call out, respond in kind, but dies
A little bit instead, the wind too cold
To bear, retreats inside the heated bar.

Lost For Good, Pass Through

In retrospect I should have raised my voice
To make a point, once back inside again,
But feared that fellowship (so few remained)
Would find my musings strange, to say not just
That night, a strike to clear the narrow streets,
But other nights as well foretell by fits
And starts a bathos mocking all decorum.
Promises of height sink back into
Obscurity, indebtedness, once funds
Have wavered, petered out. The founders come
To suit the opportunist's plank, who finds
No heroes worthy mid the living ranks.

These degradations leave the poet stressed
And questioning their thrust: so short a lease,
No matter what enthusiasms rise
From him, his musings have been battered, sapped
Beneath these weighty heights, such mighty walls,
But ultimately insubstantial, lost,
Decaying or demolished. In my youth
I walked down here & drew the world I saw,
But older now, the truth cries out for words.
I pass beneath these glass & granite wastes,
And think of cutthroat orgies, quarries mined
Up north, great mountainsides reduced to pits
To raise these towers, as *St. Peter*'s rose
While *Caracalla* & the *Colosseum*
Suffered gutting. Sun cannot get through,
The air grows thick enough to smother one
Who pines within this shade, who would conceive

Some worthier ascent, whose sense of place
Is not diminished by the vanishings,
The next development to rise & fall.
He plants his feet surveying, sees from here
A neighborhood, years down the road, a place
To dwell on fitting words, not just the thought
Of prospects narrowing, the push & shove,
Impatient offerings, but folks unrushed;
Not just these valleys of affliction, flights
Of haughty reach, beyond, above the means
Of one too poor to take a cab, whose wealth
Is in his walking mind, awake, whose debts
Will hound him to his death, but such a place
As lends an order to these arguments
He overhears within, & all those voices
Silencing his mind, surrounding him,
Until he knows he's lost for good: pass through
Unseen, unwept, you are a ludicrous
Descendent of this shore. You hear yourself
Begin to swear aloud, I pledge like Scrooge,
A renovated man for all the ghosts
He met that night, to make all three, the past,
The present, & the future, thrive in me,
My captive's ransom vested in this gift
Of love, if wrapped but meanly, still, alive,
Compounding ventured interest, as an
Avuncular inheritance that starts
Once dust's on toys, wish-lists disintegrate,
A boy sets out to earn his origins.

The Prints Fulfilled

I know those up are thrusting down to keep
Their status sure, those down must pine away,
Their wish to undermine those powers, see
Them tried, & wanting, overthrown. Nobody
Isn't striving, forced to serve or serving
Force to squeeze a living from this stone.
Head over heels, fired, raised, unsure?
I watch the glossy speculators shake
A stage of glassy offices, evict
The unlamented history, short sell,
A plaque, or less, a faded scrawl to tell
What lies below, left islanded amid
This overwhelming shade, you'll notice if
You chance to look. If you have ever felt
Alone to death down here, then heard a voice
Within defy that fear, your suffering
Will not have been the cry of vanity,
But harsh restraint, true veneration. You
Have found your understanding: devastation's
Never over, nor the renovation,
Futures sprouting from these fretful straits,
Tall stalks. The cranes rock back & forth like cradles
Off the topmost limbs, amid the scaffolds
Cling, precariously swiveling
(Some boughs do break & crush what's in their path
Below) with beams to raise in place. Each lift
Goes hatching other stories, settled on
The prior ones, as shadows stretch beneath,
Or will, the architect on hand to pace

About & double check his scrolls, to see
His final prints fulfilled, the legacy
A skyline altered slightly once again.

The watchful catch a pendulum in swing,
Neglected works decaying, singled out,
As cutters smooth the coarsened surfaces
Of walls once worthy love, if long ignored,
Remove the grime, the crust accumulated
Over time. If watchful you may catch
This struggle waged with nothingness, the likes
Of which you wish should never cease
To call for your response, amid these haunts,
These rounds, to hear your footsteps, questioning.

Epilogue

Apostrophe from Ham to nobody,
Or you, who live & breathe Manhattan,
Fit & noble fellowship, who care:
Had I three thousand tongues I'd still prefer
Speak softly, touchy with each phrase, redress
This call with whispering responses, only
Make it very clear: I sometimes hear,
Mid taxis rattling, through terminals
Of flighty crowds, beneath the clattering
Of buried trains, the broken ornamental skin,
The onion fumes; mid hidden middens
Of *Matinecocks*, as good as deeds
Or coin to founders leveling their rounds
Down here, those shells like buried teeth;
I hear, sometimes accusingly—as in
A crisis, when I'd seek to clarify
Or dare at odds to say what even matters,
Dare respond to history, the news
That stays & won't be put aside, abides
Beneath the roar of jets, the drag on wings,
The swing of cranes, erratic knocks
From wrecking balls, *etcetera*;

Hear bedrock echo back: "Deserted… Petra."

***

Santa Barbara, Dec. 2005-September 1, 2008

Lightning Source UK Ltd.
Milton Keynes UK
UKHW012018170622
404590UK00002B/293